A COMPANION TO
The Parents' Guide to Studying and Learning

THE
High School Students'
STUDYING AND
LEARNING
HANDOUTS

A COMPANION TO

The Parents' Guide to Studying and Learning

THE STUDYING AND LEARNING HANDOUTS

High School Students'

Saundra Yancy McGuire, PhD
with Stephanie McGuire, PhD

WISE**ACTION**

WISE**ACTION**

Wise Action
201 N. Union Street, Suite 110
Alexandria, Virginia 22301
https://wiseaction.co

First Wise Action trade paperback edition April 2022.

Wise Action and design are trademarks of Wise Action Company.

Bulk purchase special discounts are available. Please make inquiries via https://studyandlearn.guide.

Interior design by Kathleen Dyson.

A Library of Congress Cataloging in Publication (CIP) Program record has been applied for.

ISBN: 979-8-9856685-6-8 (paperback)

Contents

Introduction for Parents

A Warm Welcome

If you're reading this because you've already purchased *The Parents' Guide to Studying and Learning*, welcome. It's great to see you again. But if you've come across this book another way, then please let me start by explaining a little bit about what *The High School Students' Studying and Learning Handouts* actually is.

This book is a companion resource for *The Parents' Guide to Studying and Learning*, a comprehensive guide for parents to help their children in grades 8–12 supercharge their studying and really enjoy learning. *The Parents' Guide* is based on my 40-year career as an educator and researcher, and it combines brain science principles and motivational incentives into one system designed to inspire lasting behavioral changes. Countless students have used it to transform failing grades into As and Bs.

This Book Is Designed to Be a Convenient Resource for You

Because *The Parents' Guide to Studying and Learning* leads parents through an accessible method of teaching their children the same principles and concepts that I have taught for decades, it includes many handouts and worksheets designed to help students learn the material in an active, engaging, and fun way. However, I wanted readers of the book to have an uninterrupted, straightforward story about how learning works. So, the decision was made to make most of the handouts available only on *The Parents' Guide* companion website, http://studyandlearn.guide, rather than in the book. **This book, *Handouts*, exists for any parent who prefers not to print or download the handouts and worksheets from the website.** Readers of *The Parents' Guide* are directed to read the whole book and peruse each handout at least once in order to understand the entire system before sitting down to have conversations with their child.

Every resource in this book exists, free of charge, at http://studyandlearn.guide/handouts (accessible with a purchase code included in every copy of *The Parents' Guide*). On the website, you have the option of downloading the handouts and then using e-mail (or another method) to send them to your child's laptop or tablet.

Why This Book Should Always Be Used Alongside *The Parents' Guide*

The Parents' Guide explains in detail how to use all of the resources included there and, by extension, in this book. Although some of the resources in *Handouts* might be helpful out of context, they have been designed to be used alongside conversations with your child during which you convey the concepts, principles, and concrete methods they can use to excel in school. The handouts are there to make sure that these conversations are full of "aha" moments that stick in your child's memory. *The Parents' Guide* explains step by step how to have these conversations and even offers you scripts to help you with the process.

This book is called *The High School Students' Studying and Learning Handouts* because I wanted to give student readers a sense of excitement about and ownership of the content. But this is *your* book to start with. Familiarizing yourself with its contents as you read *The Parents' Guide* will give you crucial insights that will enable you to effectively motivate your child to *use* the learning strategies that I have seen help so many students. So, after you have gone through the handouts in this book, then share *Handouts* with your child.

As I explain in *The Parents' Guide*, the material is divided into *Core Content* and *Additional Content*. The Core Content should be presented to every student, while most parents will choose only a selection of the Additional Content to deliver to their child. Because I wanted to address the learning needs of as wide a range of students as possible, I included a lot of resources. That's partly why this book has so many pages. But even if you decide to present all of these handouts to your child, *The Parents' Guide* shows you exactly how to go quickly through them during your conversations.

Reasons to Use the Website Even If You Have This Book

Even though you may have decided to purchase *Handouts*, there are still a few good reasons to visit the website. There you'll find welcome videos from me—for both you and your child—to set the tone for our fun and rewarding journey together. There is also a video for an important exercise, in case you want to have me lead your child through the exercise instead of doing it yourself. Additionally, on the website, many of the handouts with illustrations are available in color, which may make a difference to your child. Finally, if you have more than one child in the household whom you want to lead through the material, you may decide later that you want to print more handouts or download them and send them to your child's device.

You might also want to visit the website if you need additional copies of four handouts exclusively for parents that do not appear in this book. You'll already have a copy of those in *The Parents' Guide*, but if you want to print extras, you can do that on the website.

To Sum Up: Please Read This Book Alongside *The Parents' Guide* Before Giving This Book to Your Child

This introduction is addressed to you because you will read this book alongside *The Parents' Guide*, to familiarize yourself with my program and prepare for your conversations with your child. But you will ultimately share this book with your child, and it contains resources almost exclusively for them.

You'll notice I said *almost*. I have included two of the parent handouts from *The Parents' Guide* because they are useful reference tables that lay out the framework for leading your child through the learning strategies, study techniques, and motivational exercises presented in *The Parents' Guide*. Chapter 12 of that book explains exactly how to choose what content to present and how to pace it in a way that works for your family's schedule.

You're Already on the Road to Success

I'm so excited that you've decided to teach your child *how* to learn by giving them techniques that they can use for the rest of their life for studying, thinking, planning, motivating themselves, and managing their time. Thank you for allowing me to accompany you and your family on this transformative journey.

Introduction for Students

You Can Get Ready for Success

I wrote my book, *A Parents' Guide to Studying and Learning*, so that your parent or guardian can help you get ready to be more successful in school, and I want to tell you right off the bat that I know you can do this together. Whether you breezed through elementary and middle school or never quite understood why math has to include letters of the alphabet, I'm going to take you on a journey full of "aha" moments that will equip you to transform your experience of learning.

The key term is *learning strategies*. A learning strategy is just a simple change to a person's study habits or a shift in attitude that makes it possible for that person to learn more deeply and securely, with much less frustration, despair, or self-punishment. These powerful learning strategies will forever change the way you think about yourself and your learning abilities.

Why Handouts?

I've included more than 50 handouts—many of them optional—in my program so that you can *actively* learn the information in this book together with your parent or guardian after they have finished reading *The Parents' Guide to Studying and Learning* alongside this book. Some of the handouts are worksheets that you get to fill out or do activities with. The idea is to give you an engaging, interactive experience similar to what would happen if you attended one of my workshops.

The other purpose of the handouts is to give you something concrete to hold onto and refer to long after your conversations with your parent or guardian are over. By the time you are finished with this book, you will have your own booklet of material, including several pages of planning and study tools. This booklet could be as short as 20 pages or as long as 60 pages, depending on what you need.

I Promise that by the Time You Finish this Book You Will:

- Understand why you may not be doing as well as you could in school.

- Know why something called *metacognition* can be such a game changer.

- Transform your thinking and learning so that it is both skillful and joyful.

- Be prepared to see your grades rise.

A Warm Welcome

At this point, please head over to the website and watch the introduction video I've recorded for you at www.studyandlearn.guide/mcguire-videos.

Handouts for Chapters 3–12, *The Parents' Guide to Studying and Learning*

HANDOUT 3.1	Who Is Dr. McGuire and Why Should I Care About What She Says?

You might care about what Dr. McGuire has to say because many students across the country have used her method to enjoy school more and get better grades. Meet Jennie and David, two students who had overnight success with her strategies:

> Hello,
>
> I am **Jennie K**_____! I attended your presentation at the _____ School. I would like to tell you that on the day you came **I got a 79.2 on my Physics test**. The test is two parts, so that **night I went home and studied using your strategies. Today I took the second part and got a 90.**
>
> Thanks,
> Jennie K.
> 9th grade

> My son, **David**, currently attends _____ HS. Three weeks ago, my son received **a 72 on his test for Honors Biology**. Yesterday, **I told him to follow your strategy** on his next test which was scheduled for today. **David received an 86 on his test today**!!! He was so relieved and grateful for the advice. Thank you so much!!
>
> —Mandrell B.

Dr. McGuire has also worked with many first-year college students who she helped go from making Ds and Fs to making As and Bs. One of the students who learned the strategies in this book went from a 42% on his first college chemistry test to getting three 100s in a row.

Another went from making a 65% and a 55% on his first two tests to making a 95% on the third one. She has lots of stories like this. Now she is bringing her strategies to high school and even middle school students.

When students come to her panicked about their grades, she tells them: "**I don't care if you made a 20% on the first test. I know that you have the ability to make a 90% or higher on the next test. That's because your score on the first test doesn't mean anything about how smart you are. It only tells me that *what you did to prepare* for the first test didn't work for you. And I can teach you a way to prepare that's going to help you ace the next test.**"

Who Is Saundra Y. McGuire?

Dr. McGuire received a 2007 Presidential Award for Excellence in Mentoring in the Oval Office of the White House because she has helped so many students reach their potential in school! For the past 30 years, she has traveled the country talking to students and teachers and helping them get better at teaching, studying, and learning. She also knows what it's like to feel lost and inadequate in school, and she wants to help you overcome those feelings the way that she and lots of her students have.

Dr. McGuire is also an expert who knows what she is talking about. She holds a PhD in chemical education and is a decorated member of some of the most important organizations relating to her work—an association of chemists, one of scientists, and another of learning specialists. Before her retirement in 2013, she was a chemistry faculty member and learning center director at Cornell University and at Louisiana State University (LSU). For the past 20 years, she has been traveling around the world, talking to people about learning.

Please go to https://www.studyandlearn.guide/mcguire-videos to hear her say hello to you.

HANDOUT 3.2   **What is Metacognition and How Can It Help Me?**

Metacognition is simply *thinking* about thinking. In other words, it's taking a step back from your automatic thinking processes and putting your attention on them in order to have more awareness about what you are doing. With that extra awareness, you can improve the ways you think and solve problems. Metacognition is like having a big brain outside of your brain looking at what your brain is doing.

Metacognition is:

1. **The ability to think about my own thinking.**

2. **The ability to recognize that I have the power to solve problems by myself.**

3. **The ability to decide how to think through a question or problem. As a result, I can change my approach if what I'm doing isn't working.**

4. **The ability to accurately judge how well I have learned something.**

Count the Vowels

Dollar bill	Cat lives
Dice	Bowling pins
Tricycle	Football team
Four-leaf clover	Dozen eggs
Hand	Unlucky Friday
Six-pack	Valentine's Day
Seven-Up	Quarter hour
Octopus	

COUNT THE VOWELS—RECALL

_____

_____

_____

_____

_____

_____

_____

Number correct _____

Score _____

COUNT THE VOWELS—RECALL #2

_____   _____

_____   _____

_____   _____

_____   _____

_____   _____

_____   _____

_____   _____

Number correct _____

Score _____

HANDOUT 3.4   Metacognition Worksheet

1. What is a three-word definition of *metacognition*? (See Handout 3.2.)

    _____

2. What are the four parts of the more in-depth definition of *metacognition*? (See Handout 3.2.)

    _____

    _____

    _____

    _____

3. Choose the **four** correct answers.

    The term *metacognition* describes:

    1. Thinking, "Hmm, I don't think I understand the themes in this book that my English teacher assigned. I'd better have a closer look."

    2. Thinking about my friend's thinking.

    3. A cartoon of a big brain watching a smaller brain do push-ups.

    4. Being able to stop in the middle of solving a problem and go in a different direction.

    5. Being able to figure out how to answer a question by myself.

    6. Spending five minutes studying geometry proofs and deciding I'm ready for the test even though I was really confused in class during the entire unit.

    7. Asking my teacher to help me with something before I've thought about how to do it.

    8. Thinking about my own thinking.

4. Review the four parts of the definition of *metacognition* on Handout 3.2. Then explain how metacognition can help a student be more independent.

    _____

    _____

    _____

5. Explain how metacognition can help a student be more creative in their problem solving.

_____

_____

_____

6. Explain how metacognition helps students become more confident.

_____

_____

_____

7. Have you ever had the experience of believing you did well on a test, an essay, or a project only to get it back with a terrible grade at the top? (This has happened to Dr. McGuire, both her children, and countless students she knows.) Explain how metacognition might help prevent surprises like that in the future. If you need a hint, see the fourth part of the definition of _metacognition_ on Handout 3.2.

_____

_____

8. Do you believe that failing the first test in a class means a student is not capable of making an A in the class? Why or why not?

_____

_____

_____

_____

HANDOUT 4.1 **Answering Reflection Questions**

1. Answer to reflection question # 1: _____

   _____

   _____

   _____

   _____

   _____

   _____

   _____

2. Answer to reflection question #2: _____

3. Answer to reflection question #3: _____

4. Answer to reflection question #4: _____

5. Before now, I've have mostly needed to be at _____

6. Right now, I mostly need to be at _____

- Studying is memorizing information for the exam; learning is when I understand it and can apply it.

- Studying is short-term; learning is long-term.

- Studying is like being force-fed a plate of yucky food; learning is like standing in front of a buffet and being able to pick my favorite foods.

- Studying is what I do the night before a test to get a good grade. Learning is what I do if I know I'm going to have to use that information later on.

- Studying is focusing on the "whats," but learning is focusing on the "hows," "whys," and "what ifs." If I focus on the "whats," then I often forget them. But if I focus on the "hows," "whys," and "what ifs," then I can recreate the "whats." For example, if I memorize history dates, then I don't remember them. But if I know the context, then I can figure out the dates. Or if I try to memorize the locations of ancient cities, I have trouble. But if I remember that cities are located near waterways because of transportation needs, then that helps me to remember where they are.

HANDOUT 4.3	Other Students' Answers to Reflection Question #3: Would You Work Harder to Make an A on a Test or Teach the Material to the Whole Class without Notes?

Answers from students who would work harder to teach the material

- Well, I have to really know it if I have to teach it!

- If I'm going to teach it, I have to think of questions I might be asked and make sure I can answer them. I don't want to look stupid in front of the class.

- I want to make sure everybody understands and is prepared for the test, so I need to figure out how to explain the information in more than one way. I might need to make charts or diagrams.

HANDOUT 4.4	Alternative Answers to Reflection Question #3: Would You Work Harder to Make an A on a Test or Teach the Material to the Whole Class without Notes?

Answers from students who would work harder to make an A

- Well, if I want to make an A, I need to master all the angles. So I would read all of the information several times, do all of the problems at the back of the chapter, and re-work any problems I missed on previous quizzes. But to teach it, I would just have to make outlines and read from some notecards.

- It's my grade, so I'm going to care more about it than everyone else's grades.

The student who wants to "master all the angles" is actually on the right track. But students who give an answer like the last one usually change their minds when they hear how other students would prepare to teach the material to the class.

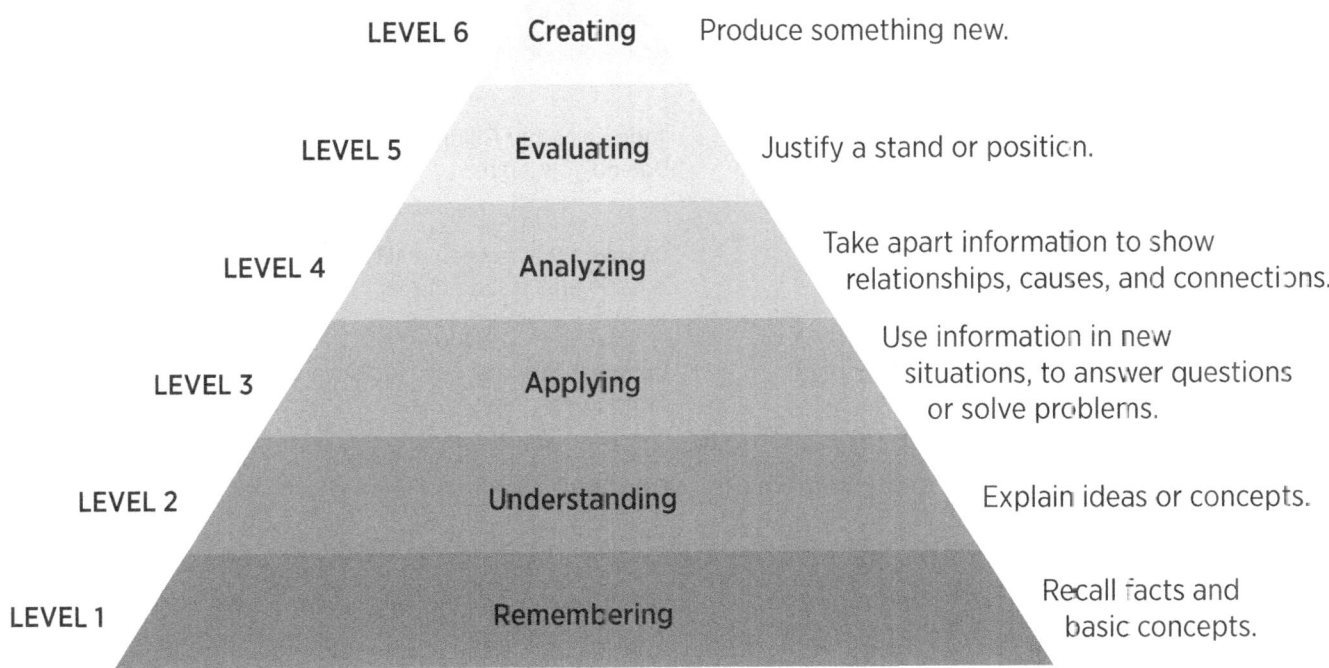

LEVEL 6	**Creating**	Produce something new.
LEVEL 5	**Evaluating**	Justify a stand or position.
LEVEL 4	**Analyzing**	Take apart information to show relationships, causes, and connections.
LEVEL 3	**Applying**	Use information in new situations, to answer questions or solve problems.
LEVEL 2	**Understanding**	Explain ideas or concepts.
LEVEL 1	**Remembering**	Recall facts and basic concepts.

This diagram of Bloom's Levels of Learning goes from the lowest level, *Remembering* (or memorizing), to the highest level, *Creating*. The text in the boxes to the right of the levels explains what each level involves. You can see that the requirements get tougher as you go from bottom to top. Many of my students approach reaching higher levels of learning the way they think of reaching higher levels of a video game. It's fun!

HANDOUT 4.6 Bloom's Levels of Learning—Goldilocks Edition

Example

Bloom's Levels of Learning

Applied to "Goldilocks and the Three Bears"

Creating — **Write** a story about Goldilocks and the Three Fish. How would it differ from Goldilocks and the Three Bears?

Evaluating — **Judge** whether Goldilocks was good or bad. Defend your opinion.

Analyzing — **Compare** this story to reality. What events could not really happen?

Applying — **Demonstrate** what Goldilocks would use if she came to your house.

Understanding — **Explain** why Goldilocks liked Baby Bear's chair the best.

Remembering — **List** the items used by Goldilocks while she was in the bears' house.

Adapted, and used by permission, from *Practicing College Learning Strategies* by Carolyn H. Hopper (Cengage Learning, 2015).

Use the Study Cycle to get the most out of in-class time and structure your out-of-class time.

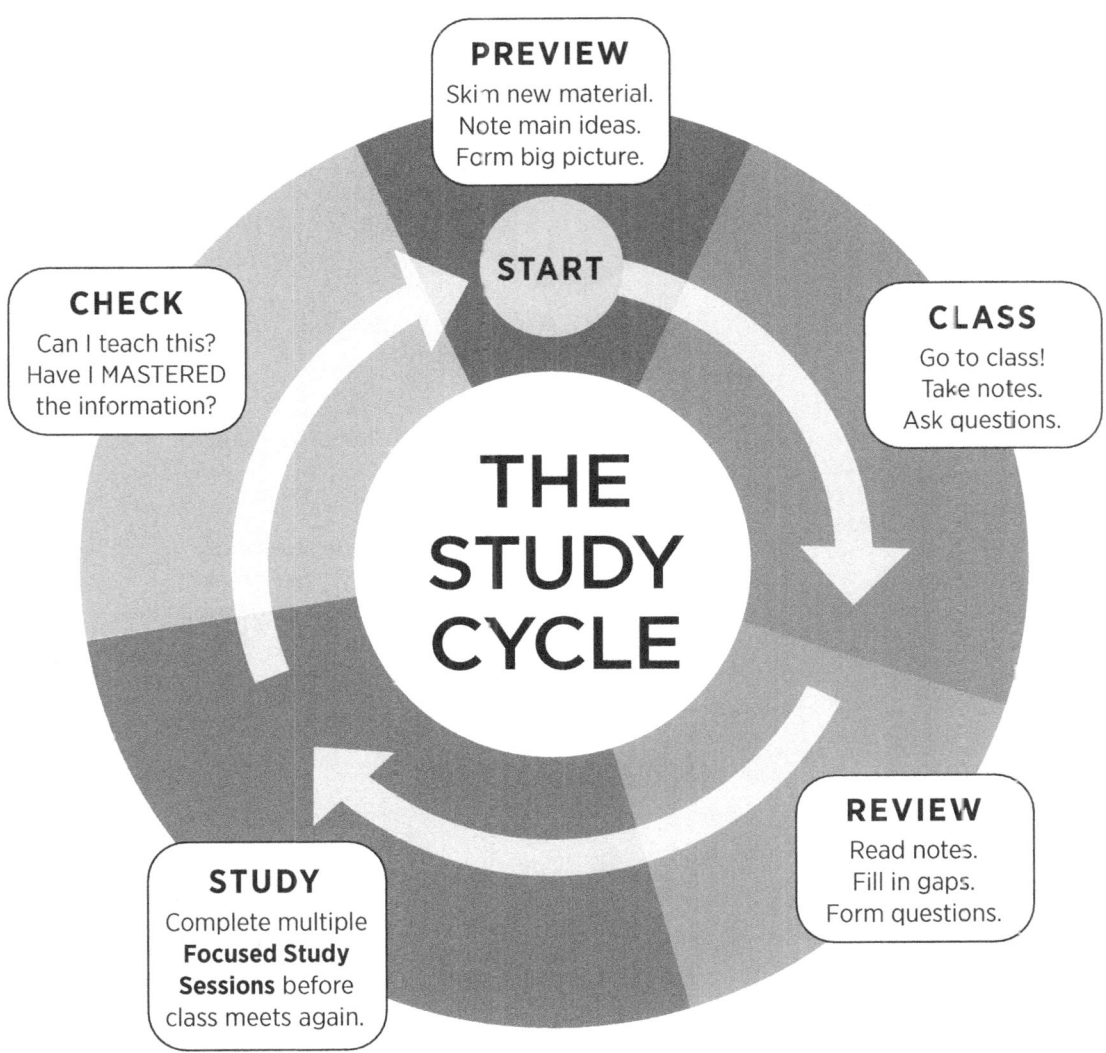

Adapted from Frank Christ's PLRS system.

FOCUSED STUDY SESSION

Schedule as many study sessions as needed to master the material.

▶ Set a specific goal.

▶ Use metacognitive learning strategies to deeply engage with the material by using concept maps, reading for comprehension, working problems and more.

▶ Remember to think critically by asking: *Why? How? What if?*

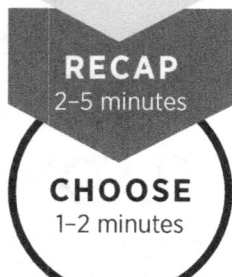

▶ Step away. Clear your mind.

▶ Summarize. Wrap up.

Continue studying?
Take a longer break?
Change tasks or subjects?

SHORTER

INTERMEDIATE

LONGER

Adapted from Frank Christ's PLRS system.

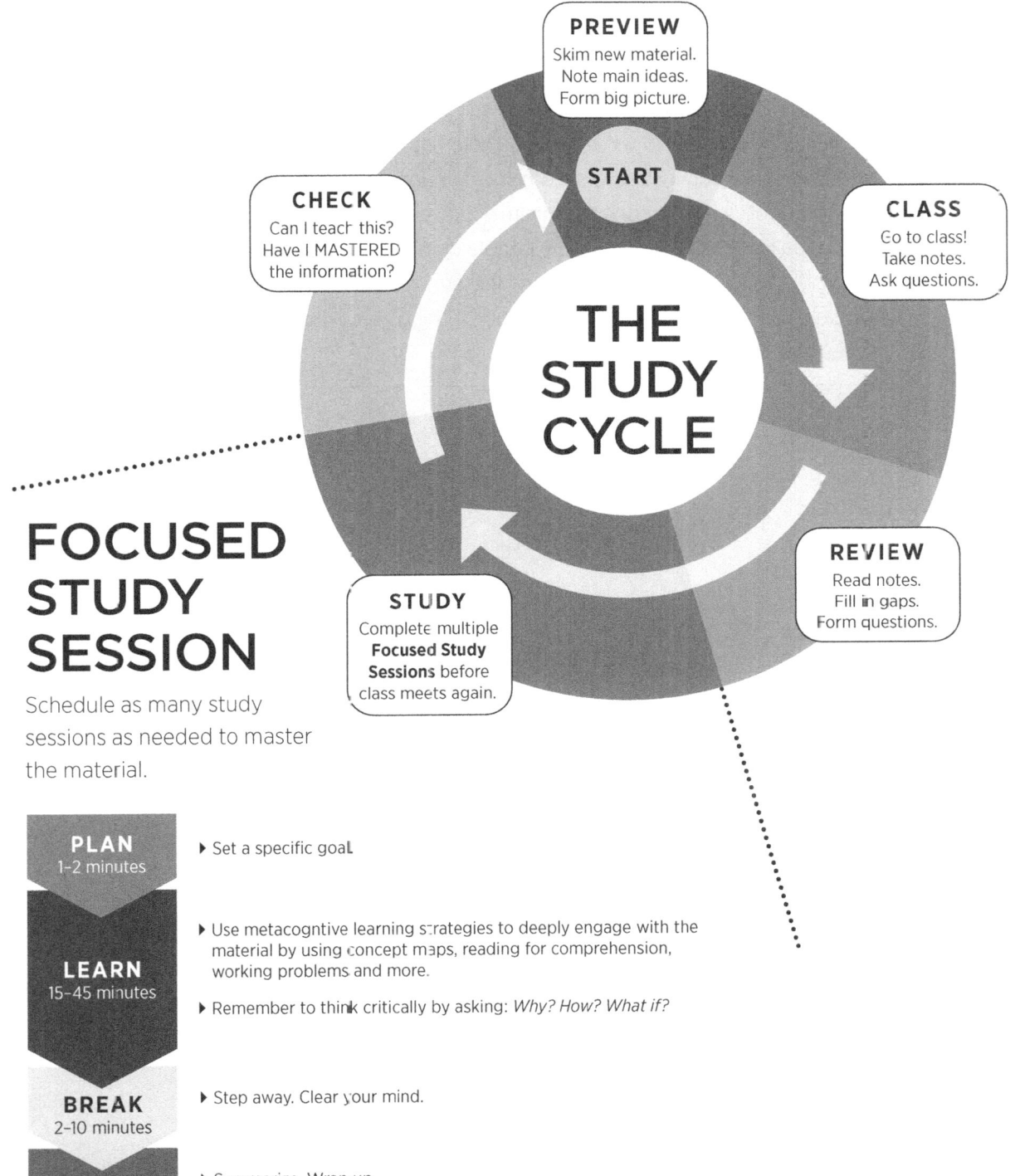

THE STUDY CYCLE

PREVIEW
Skim new material.
Note main ideas.
Form big picture.

START

CLASS
Go to class!
Take notes.
Ask questions.

REVIEW
Read notes.
Fill in gaps.
Form questions.

STUDY
Complete multiple
**Focused Study
Sessions** before
class meets again.

CHECK
Can I teach this?
Have I MASTERED
the information?

FOCUSED STUDY SESSION

Schedule as many study sessions as needed to master the material.

PLAN
1–2 minutes
▸ Set a specific goal.

LEARN
15–45 minutes
▸ Use metacognitive learning strategies to deeply engage with the material by using concept maps, reading for comprehension, working problems and more.
▸ Remember to think critically by asking: *Why? How? What if?*

BREAK
2–10 minutes
▸ Step away. Clear your mind.

RECAP
2–5 minutes
▸ Summarize. Wrap up.

CHOOSE
1–2 minutes
Continue studying?
Take a longer break?
Change tasks or subjects?

HANDOUT 6.1   Guess the Activity

Read the following paragraph and try to guess what activity the text is describing.

A newspaper is better than a magazine. A seashore is a better place than the street. At first it is better to run than walk. You may have to try several times. It takes some skill, but it is easy to learn. Even young children can enjoy it. Once successful, complications are minimal. Birds seldom get too close. Rain, however, soaks in very fast. Too many people doing the same thing can also cause problems. One needs lots of room. If there are no complications, it can be very peaceful. A rock will serve as an anchor. If things break loose from the rock, however, you will not get a second chance.

The Power of Previewing

FLYING KITES

A newspaper is better than a magazine. A seashore is a better place than the street. At first it is better to run than walk. You may have to try several times. It takes some skill, but it is easy to learn. Even young children can enjoy it. Once successful, complications are minimal. Birds seldom get too close. Rain, however, soaks in very fast. Too many people doing the same thing can also cause problems. One needs lots of room. If there are no complications, it can be very peaceful. A rock will serve as an anchor. If things break loose from the rock, however, you will not get a second chance.

Do you see that the heading of the paragraph helps you make sense of the text, which probably seemed like nonsense before you read the heading? This exercise gives you an idea of what happens when you take five to ten minutes before class to preview what will be covered in class.

Previewing is taking your assigned reading and looking at all of the headings, bold words, italicized words underlined words, and images like charts, graphs, tables, photographs, or other visual aids. Knowing that the paragraph on this page is about kites helped you to make sense of it. In the same way, having an idea of what will be covered in class makes it easier for you to digest what the teacher is saying, stay engaged in class, and ask questions as they arise instead of discovering confusion later at home or on a test. *Previewing is powerful! And it only takes five to ten minutes.*

HANDOUT 6.2   Using Homework to Test Your Understanding

PHASE 1: Study your notes and reading assignments as well as you can *before* you do your homework. While you are studying, if you come across any example problems or end-of-section questions in your reading assignments, do them *without* looking at the solutions.

Procedure for Doing Problems or Questions without Looking at Notes or Solutions:

1. Focus only on the first step of the problem or question.

2. Set a timer for three minutes, and do your best brainstorming until the timer goes off. If you finish before three minutes is up, move on to step 5.

3. If you're not done with the first step of the problem or question after the timer goes off, but you're making progress, then reset the timer for another three minutes and keep going until you finish that step, resetting the timer as many times as it takes, or until you get stuck.

4. If at any point you get thoroughly stumped for a whole three minutes, or you just can't take it anymore, then go ahead and look at your notes, but only the notes that help you solve *the first step*.

5. Once that first step of the problem is done, move on to the second step . Do it exactly the way you just did the first step.

6. After you've finished the second step, move on to the third step, and keep going until you finish the question, problem, or process.

7. If there is a solution available, compare your final answer to the solution. If they aren't the same, set your timer and see if you can figure out where you went wrong.

    ▪ During this procedure, if you start to feel unsettled or worried at any point, remember that those feelings are normal, and take a few deep, slow breaths.

    ▪ If you find the timer distracting or unhelpful at any point, you don't have to use it. It's only there so you know the problem won't go on forever.

PHASE 2: Now turn to your homework and do the assigned questions or problems without looking at your notes or reading. See the procedure above. If you approach your homework using this method, then every single time you do homework, you'll be training yourself to ace your next test.

Bonus Strategy: Combine Learning Strategies #5 and #6

Be the Teacher *and* Use Homework to Test Your Understanding

PHASE 1: Study your notes and reading assignments as well as you can *before* you do your homework. While you are studying, if you come across any example problems or end-of-section questions in your reading assignments, do them *without* looking at the solutions.

PHASE 2: Teach the material you've just learned to an empty chair, a stuffed animal, an imaginary classroom, your reflection in the mirror, or whatever you want until you can do it confidently.

PHASE 3: Turn to your homework and do the assigned questions or problems without looking at your notes or reading.

HANDOUT 6.3   Ten Learning Strategies

1. **Preview** (read headings, subheadings; bold, italicized, and underlined text; and all images or graphics).

2. **Come up with questions the reading might answer.**

3. **Put what you are reading into your own words.** (Paraphrasing: see below.)

4. **Use the right study tools to understand reading assignments.**
    (See the list of study tools on Handout 6.5; see also below.)

5. **Use homework to test your understanding (Handout 6.2).**

6. **Be the teacher** (teach the material out loud to an empty chair, a stuffed animal, action figure, invisible class, etc.).

7. **Participate in class and take notes.**

8. **Always go for 100% understanding.**

9. **Use the Study Cycle with Focused Study Sessions (Handout 5.3).**

10. **Study with a friend or two if it works for you.**

A Deeper Look at Strategy #3: Put What You Are Reading into Your Own Words

Do the following for each section of your reading assignments:

Read the first paragraph, and then put that paragraph into your own words, either out loud or in your head. Then read the second paragraph and put it into your own words *as you also fold in information from paragraph 1*, again, either out loud or in your head. Then read the third paragraph and put it into your own words, *as you also fold in information from paragraphs 1 and 2*. Repeat until the end of the section. When the next section begins, start fresh with only the first paragraph of that section.*

A Deeper Look at Strategy #4: Use the Right Study Tools to Understand Reading Assignments

Handout 6.5 lists a range of tools you can choose from. I just want you to know that if you find it distracting to write things down *while* you are reading, you can always wait until you've gotten to the end of a section, or a whole chapter, to start making your flashcards, maps, or notes—as long as you have been doing your paraphrasing all along the way. But if it works better for you to write things down as you read, then definitely do it that way.

---

*You can replace this method with something called SQ3R (survey, question, read, recite, review), SQ4R (survey, question, read, respond, record, review), or SQ5R (survey, question, read, recite, record, review, reflect) if that's what your teacher uses.

HANDOUT 6.4   **Learning Strategies Worksheet**

Feel free to consult any of the handouts you have received so far in order to answer any of the following questions:

1. What should you look for when you preview? About how long should it take?

   _____

   _____

2. Why is it important to preview? How does previewing change your ability to learn?

   _____

   _____

3. Which strategy can you use to make yourself more interested in doing a reading assignment?

   _____

   _____

4. What is paraphrasing, and why is it more effective than copying?

   _____

   _____

5. Explain Dr. McGuire's paraphrasing method in your own words.

   _____

   _____

6. Why is it ineffective to do your homework while following along with examples in your notes or the book?

_____

_____

7. Describe another way of doing your homework that helps you learn the material much better than just following along with examples.

_____

_____

8. Name three benefits of doing your homework this way.

_____

_____

_____

9. When you use the strategy of teaching the material out loud, what or who would you like to use as your "student"? Give as many options as you would enjoy using.

_____

_____

10. Give two benefits of going to class and taking notes.

_____

_____

11. Give two benefits of aiming for 100% mastery.

_____

_____

12. Why is it important to use the Study Cycle with Focused Study Sessions? What could happen if you stop using them?

_____

_____

13. Is studying with friends productive for you? _____

14. If you answered yes to question #13, list a few friends you'd like to be in *learn mode* with.

_____

_____

Even using just one of these tools during your Focused Study Sessions could transform your learning! Try as many as you feel excited about, or others that teachers or friends suggest.

1. FLASHCARDS

Flashcards are perfect for memorizing information like vocabulary words, names, dates, geographical facts, and formulas.

2. NOTE-TAKING

As you use the reading strategy of putting what you read into your own words (see Handout 6.3: Ten Learning Strategies), you can *write down* some or all of those words. As you follow the strategy and make progress through a section, you would only need to add *new* information and insights to your written notes, even though you would continue to paraphrase from the beginning of the section.

Another option for note-taking is traditional outlining, using roman numerals (I, II, III) to represent main ideas, the letters (A, B, C) to represent aspects of each main idea, and numbers (1, 2, 3) to represent details of each aspect of a main idea.

Other ideas appear in Appendix B: Study Tools Guide.

3. HIGHLIGHTING

If your reading assignments are online or digital, it is often possible to highlight the text in different colors. If you are reading books or handouts, and you know you definitely have permission to mark them up, then you can use highlighter pens or pencils of different colors. Color coding can be an efficient way to remind yourself how information is organized into different categories. One note of caution: don't use highlighting as a way of passively marking information "to learn later on." Instead, use it to actively support your use of the reading strategies.

4. MIND MAPS, CHARTS, GRAPHS, TABLES, AND TIMELINES

Using images can be a powerful way for some people to engage in deep learning. A mind map is created by placing a central concept or topic in the center of the map and drawing branches from the central topic to several main ideas about it. As for charts, graphs, tables, and timelines, you have probably already seen many of them in school on the board or in your class assignments. You can create them, too, in order to learn information actively and securely. Examples and more information are given in Appendix B: Study Tools Guide.

5. STUDY GUIDES

Study guides are great for reviewing information that you have learned over a period of weeks or months while using the other tools. Two popular formats for a study guide are outlines and tables (sometimes called charts). An example is given in Appendix B: Study Tools Guide.

6. MNEMONIC DEVICES

A *mnemonic* (nuh-MAHN-ic) *device* is just a fancy term for a trick that helps you remember something. The name Roy G. Biv is one example. It represents the colors of the rainbow: Red, Orange, Yellow, Green, Blue, Indigo, and Violet. The first letter of each of the colors spells Roy G. Biv. Here is a second example: Dear King Philip Came Over for Great Spaghetti. The first letter of each word in the sentence matches the first letter of each of the taxonomic levels that biology students have to learn (domain, kingdom, phylum, class, order, family, genus, species). The nonsense word IPMAT can help you remember the phases of mitosis: interphase, prophase, metaphase, anaphase, and telophase. Whenever you have to memorize a list of some kind, see if you can come up with a mnemonic device to help you.

7. HOMEMADE PRACTICE QUIZZES AND TESTS

You can use past homework assignments, quizzes, and extra textbook questions to try to create your own practice test. This is an advanced study strategy, but it can work really well. If you decide not to use this study tool, no worries. However, as long as you do your homework in the way that I've suggested, you will be regularly testing yourself.

Tip: Keep it simple and focus on one to three tools that you feel excited about. Just one of these tools, used with the learning strategies, could transform your learning!

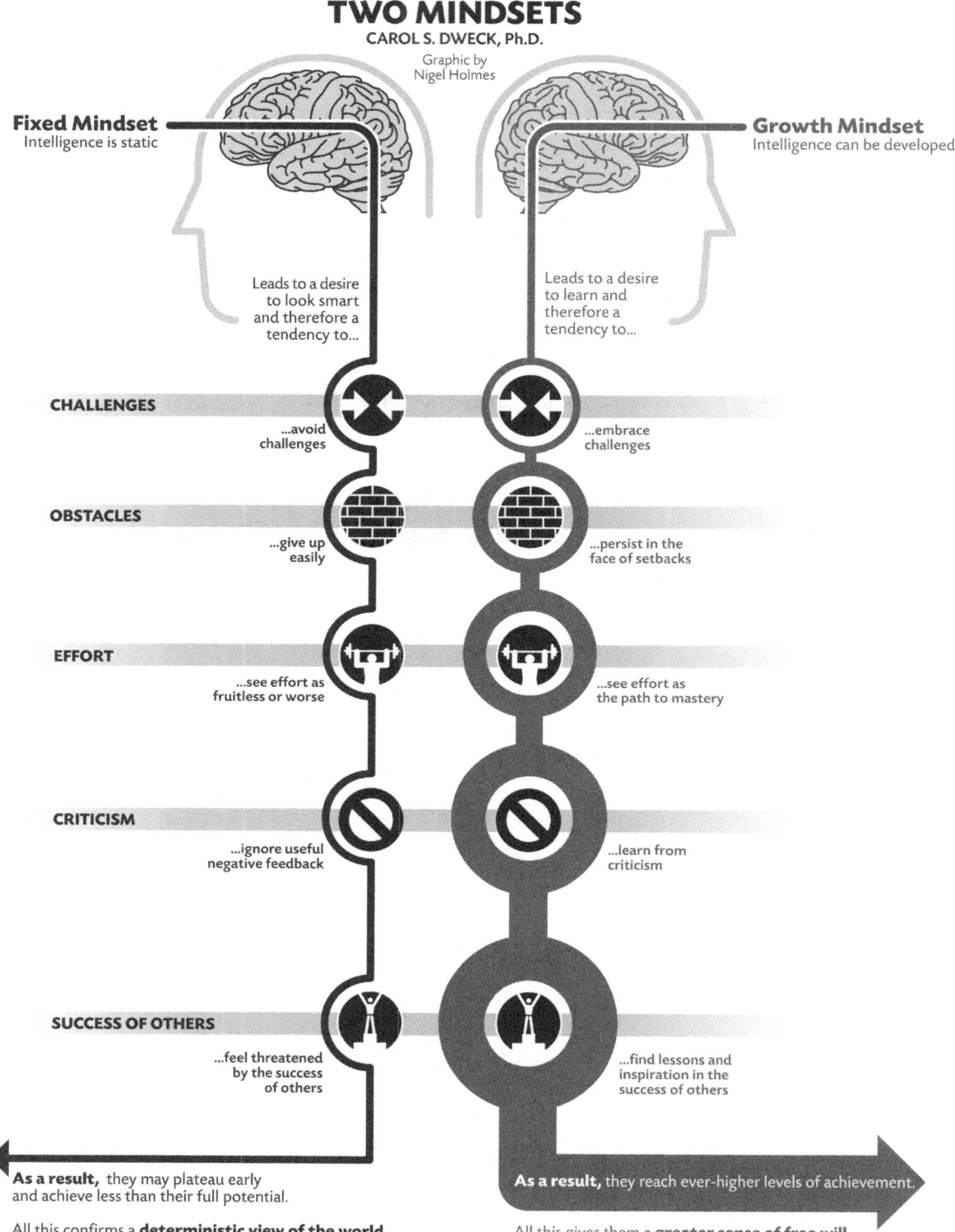

Used by permission from *Mindset: The New Psychology of Success* by Carol S. Dweck (Ballentine, 2007).

HANDOUT 7.2   **Mindset Worksheet**

1. Retrieve Handout 7.1: Fixed and Growth Mindsets. Use the information on the handout to fill in the following chart, and contrast the characteristics of fixed and growth mindsets. Which would you rather have?

CHARACTERISTICS OF A FIXED MINDSET	CHARACTERISTICS OF A GROWTH MINDSET

I would rather have a _____ mindset because _____

_____

2. Has there ever been a time in your life when you responded to criticism or negative feedback with a determination to improve?

_____

_____

3. Did you improve? _____

4. Has there ever been a time in your life when you decided to give up on an activity that you enjoyed because someone else said you weren't very good at it or gave you negative feedback?

_____

_____

5. What was the difference between the activities in question 2 and question 4? Why did you keep going with the first activity?

_____

_____

_____

6. Before today, would you say you had more of a fixed mindset or a more of a growth mindset?

_____

_____

7. True or False: For many students, grades primarily reflect past behavior rather than talent or ability.

_____

8. Are grades always a reflection of your potential? If not, what do grades show?

_____

_____

9. Do you believe your current ability or your future behavior will determine your grades in the future? Why?

_____

_____

_____

10. Do you believe you will be smarter in five years than you are right now? In one year? In a month? Explain.

_____

_____

_____

11. What is the biological basis of the idea that intelligence can grow? What can brain cells do?

_____

_____

_____

Handout 8.1 is a parent worksheet and only appears in *The Parents' Guide to Studying and Learning*

HANDOUT 8.2   My Interests and Things I Enjoy Doing

It's perfectly fine if you don't know the answers to some of these questions. This worksheet is only meant to be a fun brainstorming activity for you.

1. List your interests and hobbies, things that light you up inside or that you really look forward to doing.

_____

_____

_____

2. Do you have any ideas about what you might want to do when you're an adult? Dream as big as you want to and also list some things that feel more realistic.

Dream jobs: _____

_____

_____

Jobs I would enjoy that may be more practical: _____

_____

_____

Many people end up doing more than one job during the course of their lives. The point of having you list more realistic jobs is *not* to suggest you can't make your dreams come true. But, depending on your dream job, you may need to make some steady money along the way.

HANDOUT 8.3   How Do You Prefer to Learn?

We can't always have things the way we want them. But when we can, it's important to ask ourselves what we want. The first step to discovering what we might want is to think about our preferences.

There are no right or wrong answers for this worksheet.

1. Do you prefer quieter environments with more stillness or livelier environments with more action?

     _____

2. Do you study better with silence or background noise?   _____

3. If some background noise is better for you, which kinds work for you? Which kinds don't work for you?

     _____

     _____

4. Do you enjoy working with others? Do you look forward to group projects?

     _____

5. Do you enjoy using underlining, using highlighters, or color coding your notes? If so, is that for all of your classes or just some? Which ones?

     _____

6. Do you find yourself writing down notes during class and making lots of notes while you do reading assignments? If so, is that for all of your classes or just some? Which ones?

     _____

7. Do you find images, like charts and graphs, helpful for learning? If so, is that for all of your classes or just some? Which ones?

     _____

8. Do you find listening to information, like in a podcast, helpful for remembering it? If so, is that for all of your classes or just some? Which ones?

     _____

9. Do you find videos helpful for learning? If so, is that for all of your classes or just some? Which ones?

     _____

10. When you are trying to think about something complicated, do you try to think about it point by point (making a list in your mind), or do you imagine more of a map (with the different parts of the problem having relationships with each other in space)? Or do you do both? Or something different altogether?

_____

_____

11. Do you enjoy labs and field trips more than in-class learning? _____

This worksheet should give you an idea of the kinds of learning activities you prefer. If you answered yes to question 5, making flashcards may be a great study tool for you. If for question 9, you tend to visualize maps, then concept mapping (or mind mapping) might work very well for you. If you answered yes to question 7, then recording information and listening back to it could be useful for you. If you answered yes to question 10, you may want to do active things as you study, like reenacting historical battles or court cases, acting out the plot of a novel, or mimicking the activity of an electron in orbitals of different shapes.

However you learn best, you should try to make your learning activities as close to your preferences as you can, so that you will have the most fun learning. Keep in mind that having preferences doesn't mean that you *can't* learn in other ways. Pizza might be your favorite food, but you still like sandwiches, and you can also eat your least favorite foods whenever you have to. In other words, you *can* learn under most conditions. It's just that, when you have a choice, why not make life as fun as possible?

Whatever you choose, definitely use The Study Cycle (Handout 5.3) in addition to the teaching strategy and the homework strategy (strategies #5 and #6 on Handout 6.3)!

Just one more question before you're finished with this worksheet:

Here are the top three things that would make it much easier for me to do my best in school and enjoy learning:

1. _____

2. _____

3. _____

Remember that because we're always growing and changing, our preferences can change too! It can be interesting to look back and see all the ways we have changed. For example, I used to dread word problems, but I learned to love them after I learned the right strategy for doing them.

After you finish this worksheet, share it with your parent or mentor so that they can support you in doing the things you prefer as often as possible.

HANDOUT 8.4 **How to Figure Out What You Are Actually Supposed to Be Doing**

Have you ever looked at an assignment and thought, *"Wait, now what? What exactly am I actually supposed to be doing here? What does the teacher want from me?"* This is a universal experience. Adults go through the same thing at their jobs sometimes, wondering what a boss or a client expects of them. Fortunately, there are concrete steps you can take to figure out the answers you need.

STEP 1:

Gather all of the materials that tell you what the assignment is supposed to be.

This may include your class syllabus, which is the document the teacher may have given you at the very beginning of the year that lays out the class plan for the whole year. There may also be specific handouts or online documents for that assignment, as well as class notes you took while the teacher was explaining it. Gather all of that material and read it carefully. It might help to make brief notes about the important points, like, for example, "Chapters 8–12, 1,000 words, different rulers during Ming dynasty, due 4/12."

STEP 2:

If you are still confused about what you should be doing, and there is still time, **respectfully ask your teacher for clarification.**

Begin by sharing what you *have* figured out and ask about the specific things you are confused about. For example, "Ms. Jones, I get that we're supposed to write 1,000 words on how different emperors ruled during the Ming dynasty, but I don't understand how many emperors we have to write about."

To really impress your teacher, come up with possible answers to your questions and ask if it's okay for you to do that. For example, if you only want to write about two emperors, you could ask, "Ms. Jones, I get that we're supposed to write 1,000 words on how different emperors ruled during the Ming dynasty, but I just wanted to ask you—is it okay if I only write about Hongwu and Jiajing?" Not only do you make your teacher's job easier and demonstrate that you have invested time and thoughtfulness in the assignment, but you also get another opportunity to ask for what you want.

STEP 3:

If there isn't enough time to ask your teacher, then contact a friend who is likely to know the answer. You shouldn't have to do this more than once or twice because in the future, you will begin your assignments early enough to be able to ask the teacher if you need to. You will also begin to notice when you need clarification, even as the assignment is first being given.

STEP 4:

Now that you know what you should be doing, **break the task down into smaller steps**.

For a term paper, your breakdown might look like this:

Term Paper Breakdown

1. Brainstorm and think about a main idea

2. Gather primary and secondary sources

3. Do active reading and make notes

4. Outline

5. Write first draft

6. Revise

Sometimes you'll realize that a step in your breakdown needs to be broken down even further when you get to it. For example, the breakdown of step 3, "Do active reading and make notes," might be:

Step 3 Breakdown

1. Chapter 8 from textbook

2. *Letters to a Young Poet* by Rainer Maria Rilke

3. *A Ringing Glass: A Biography of Rainer Maria Rilke* by Donald Prater

4. Class notes

As you can see, each of those steps can be broken down even further. Break a task down into the smallest steps that you need in order to feel like you can tackle them successfully. Whenever my daughter, the one with the PhD, feels stuck about anything, she breaks it down. She gave me permission to share one with you. This was for a day when she was feeling particularly unsure of herself.

Overwhelm Breakdown

1. Get out of bed

2. Arrange pencils on desk

3. Open laptop and file

4. Take a deep breath

5. Break down beginning of task

The point here is that you never have to feel bad about feeling stuck or not knowing what to do. You can always break something down into steps that feel manageable for you, and if you feel like you've exhausted all your options, you can always ask for help.

HANDOUT 8.5 Self-Talk Journaling Worksheet

What is self-talk? It's just a name for the chatter most of us have running through our heads. *"Oh, I need to take out the trash. . . .Where did I put my keys? . . . Argh, socks on the floor again."* When we're trying to solve a problem, this chatter is sometimes directed at ourselves. The most helpful self-talk is kind and encouraging, but many people can have pretty negative self-talk, especially when they make mistakes. This worksheet teaches you a journaling technique to be more aware of your self-talk and to encourage it to be kinder and more helpful.

Use this journaling technique for five minutes a day, perhaps after you brush your teeth, or at a time just after you make a mistake or experience a disappointment. Or do it just before a pressure situation like a test. (Definitely do not constantly listen to your self-talk. Researchers have estimated that the average person has over 6,000 thoughts per day!)

STEP 1:

Listen to your inner voice and write down what it says. It's normal if it's negative. Don't worry about that. Example 1, below, shows this step.

STEP 2:

Think about something kind and compassionate you could say instead. Example 2, below, shows this step. The point here is not to *disagree* with the voice or try to be overly positive—like example 3, below. That will just make the negative voice want to argue back. (This is normal and happens in everyone's mind.) The point is to meet the negativity with kindness.

Example:

1. Self-talk: *I can't believe I'm so dumb. I studied so hard on that test and then made such a stupid mistake. I'll never get it right in that class.*

2. Self-compassion: *I did a good job studying so hard and getting all the things right that I got right. I'm a human being, not a robot. Sometimes I make mistakes. It's great that I enjoyed myself while studying and did as well as I did.*

3. Self-compassion attempt (LESS HELPFUL): *You're not dumb! You're smart! You're gonna rock that class so hard from now on!!*

Now you try it:

Date _____

1. Self-talk: _____

    _____

    _____

2. Self-compassion: _____

    _____

    _____

Date _____

1. Self-talk: _____

    _____

    _____

2. Self-compassion: _____

    _____

    _____

Date _____

1. Self-talk: _____

    _____

    _____

2. Self-compassion: _____

    _____

    _____

Doing What *You* Can and Letting Go of the Rest

This worksheet is about *how* we explain to ourselves *why* things happen to us. Let's say I'm leaving my office on campus one afternoon, and I get caught out in a rainstorm without my umbrella. I have some choices for *how* to explain why I got wet:

- I could say, "Oh, the stupid weather!" or "Why didn't Mr. Smith tell me that it was raining?"

- Or I could say, "Oh dear, I forgot my umbrella. I'll make sure to stick a Post-it note on my computer reminding myself to take it next time."

In other words, I can blame factors *outside* my control, or I can focus on things *within* my control. Notice that I don't blame or judge myself for forgetting the umbrella. But I do take responsibility for what I could have done to ensure a different outcome.

Here's the thing. We can't control someone else's behavior, only our own. So, if we want to have the most fun and success in life, it makes sense to focus on what *we* can do to get the results we want.

Here are two quotes from students, explaining why they did poorly on a test:*

"There were no examples of problems like the ones on the test. I have never seen these problems before. [They were] never introduced in class."

"[The teacher] went through materials fast [during class]....I didn't follow."

Do you see what is happening here? These students are blaming the teacher for their poor grades. But you can't control what the teacher does. You can only control what you do.

A more useful response might have been, "OK, I can see that the way I studied for this test didn't really work. I'll be sure to see what I did wrong and use different strategies next time."

Notice that I'm not saying that the teacher was perfect. But it's a better use of your time and energy to focus on changing *your* behavior than on trying to change someone else's. Usually, if a teacher is really out of bounds, enough people will complain about it so that you don't have to. It's faster and easier to change your behavior right away and raise your grades instead of waiting for a teacher to change their behavior.

Now take a look at what some students said about why they did well on an exam:

"I have continued to look at the effective learning strategies you introduced to the class last week. I have been going to group tutoring sessions...and they helped tremendously."

"I have taken a new approach to studying by using some of your suggestions and it does seem to be helping. By previewing the chapter before [class] and studying the notes online, I better understand the material as you go over it [in class]."

These students recognize that by taking responsibility for their actions, they have been able to succeed.

---

* Zhao, Ningfeng, Jeffrey G. Wardeska, Saundra Y. McGuire, and Elzbieta Cook. "Metacognition: An Effective Tool to Promote Success in College Science Learning." *Journal of College Science Teaching* 43, no. 4 (2014): 48–54.

We always have a choice about how to explain things to ourselves. When you are faced with a result that you didn't want, how do you explain it to yourself? Do you focus on factors that you can control, or on factors you can't control? It's normal to focus on factors you can't control. Nearly everyone does it. But as we develop and mature, we learn to shift our focus to what we can control.

Please note that I'm not asking you to ignore unhelpful things that other people may be doing. If one of the reasons you did poorly on an exam is that your sibling was playing loud music until 2 a.m. the night before, definitely ask your sibling to keep it down in the future. Always respectfully ask for what you need and want. But once you have done that, focus on the actions *you* can take to get the results you want.

1. Now list three disappointments you experienced recently:

    _____

    _____

    _____

2. For each of the three disappointments, list some factors outside your control that affected the outcome:

    _____

    _____

    _____

3. Now for each of the three disappointments, list some factors within your control that affected the outcome:

    _____

    _____

    _____

4. Focusing on the factors within your control, list some things you could have done differently to ensure an outcome you would have been happier with:

    _____

    _____

    _____

5. Do you think it will be more productive and rewarding to focus on the answers to question #4 or the answers to question #2? Explain your answer.

_____

_____

_____

Handout 9.1 is a parent worksheet and only appears in *The Parents' Guide to Studying and Learning*

HANDOUT 9.2   Dealing with Setbacks, Mistakes, and Failure

Mistakes can be good, and failure is often the best teacher. When you relate to failure this way, instead of thinking that it is wrong or shameful, you give yourself the best chance to learn, grow, and have fun.

Here are some statements about making mistakes that I've collected from students over the years:

- You learn from your mistakes.

- You can correct your mistakes.

- You never make the same mistake twice.

- You learn where your mind has a tendency to go wrong.

One well-known study* compared how two groups of students felt about mistakes. The first group of students did better on international math tests than the second group did. On average, the students from the second group felt embarrassed when they made math mistakes, while students from the first group were mostly unbothered because they were aware of the *usefulness* of math mistakes. Researchers suggested that this awareness meant that when they made mistakes, these students calmly interpreted them as a sign that they needed to go a little further with their efforts instead of interpreting them to mean that they might as well give up. This attitude toward mistakes was associated with better performance on tests. The take-home message? **Mistakes are nothing to be ashamed of. They are the path to growth and success.**

*Uttal, David H. "Beliefs about Genetic Influences on Mathematics Achievement: A Cross-Cultural Comparison." *Genetica* 99 (1997): 165–172.

HANDOUT 9.3   **Stumbling Blocks or Stepping Stones?**

I want to share with you a story about turning a failure into fuel for success. We can train ourselves to think, "I'm going to succeed *because* of this failure" instead of thinking, "I'm going to succeed *even though* I'm experiencing this failure." This philosophy is summarized by the saying, "The obstacle is the path."

Another way to say it is: **What's in the way *is* the way**.

Sydnie was a student I met near the beginning of her freshman year in college. She had done well in high school, but when I met her, **she had just gotten a 64 on her first calculus test and a 65 on her first chemistry test.** These were devastating scores for Sydnie. I could see she was heartbroken as she began sobbing across from me. I spent about an hour with her, giving her the same learning strategies that I've shared in this book. Sydnie went on to make a 95, 90, and 70 on her remaining chemistry tests. She made a 96 on the final exam and got an A in the course. In calculus, she made 100, 97, 96, and 90 on her remaining tests, and she made a 93 on the final exam. **Sydnie ended the semester with a 4.0 GPA. But if she had not almost failed her first two tests, she never would have come to me to learn the strategies she used to make a 4.0. She turned a stumbling block into a stepping stone.**

Now I'd like to tell you two more stories of people using obstacles to power their success, in the areas of performance and athletics.

My older daughter played the flute in her high school band. One summer, the band got the opportunity to participate in an international competition in Vienna, Austria, and I got to tag along as a chaperone. I remember sitting in the open-air plaza listening to the band's last concert before their competition performance. I don't know very much about music, but even I could tell that it wasn't going well. The instruments weren't playing together, things sounded out of tune, and the whole thing just sounded like fatigue and exhaustion instead of joy and harmony. The director of the band looked as dejected as the players, as the performance mercifully wound down to an end. He told the band how disappointed he was in their dismal playing before we all trudged off to the hotel.

Just before the competition the next morning, I watched the band members warming up. It was the most focused and concentrated I'd ever seen them. They seemed determined not to repeat the previous day's disaster. And do you know what? **It was the best performance they played in Vienna. They came home with a medal!** If the band hadn't encountered such a huge obstacle, they wouldn't have pulled off such a huge triumph. They turned a stumbling block into a stepping stone.

Some of you are probably sports fans. If so, you might remember the legendary NBA finals of 2016, when LeBron James and the Cleveland Cavaliers came back from the brink of defeat to win the championship, beating Stephen Curry and the Golden State Warriors. Let me back up for those you who aren't sports fans. (Full disclosure: I'm not really one either, but I heard this story and thought it was a great one to tell you.) To win the NBA finals, one team has to win at least four games against the other team. So, after four games, the Cavaliers were down 1–3, and the next game was being played in San Francisco, where the Warriors had the home-court advantage. Well, the Cavaliers just saw that stumbling block and turned it into a stepping stone! They won Game 5 in San Francisco, Game 6 in Cleveland, and then Game 7 on the Warriors' home turf to clinch the championship. **The Cavaliers became the first team in NBA history to come back from a 3-1 deficit to become champions.**

In a 2020 interview, former Cavalier Richard Jefferson was asked whether the team knew it was going to come back from a two-game deficit. He said, "No. No one knew. But you don't try and eat a big steak in one bite. You really just look at it from a standpoint of: We believe we can play better. We knew we could play better."* Indeed. No matter what challenges you're facing, believe in yourself and that you can rise to meet them, one determined step at a time.

I hope these stories convince you that not only can you turn a stumbling block into a stepping stone, but you can also turn a setback into an *advantage*.

Whenever you encounter a stumbling block, will you think to yourself, "How can I make this a stepping stone?"

---

* Jefferson, Richard. "Richard Jefferson breaks down the Cavs' 3–1 comeback in the 2016 NBA Finals" ESPN. April 2, 2020.
  https://www.youtube.com/watch?v=u1jwjlq2pA4

HANDOUT 9.4   **Mistakes and Failure Worksheet**

Discuss the answers to these questions with your parent or mentor.

MAKING MISTAKES AND FAILING

1. Is it shameful to make a mistake or to fail? Why or why not?

    _____

    _____

2. Do you think there has ever been a person who never experienced failure or the difficult feelings that come with it? Why or why not?

    _____

    _____

3. Is it possible for two people to look at the same outcome and for one of them to interpret it as a success and the other to interpret it as a failure? Can you think of an example? Why do you think this happens?

    _____

    _____

4. What are some advantages of making a mistake?

    _____

    _____

5. What are some disadvantages of being afraid to make mistakes?

    _____

    _____

6. Can there be an advantage to making a *lot* of mistakes? _____

7. What do you think would happen to someone who did not experience a significant failure until they were 13 years old?

    _____

    _____

8. What opportunities do your teachers give you to make mistakes *before* you take a test?

_____

_____

9. Is failure necessarily bad? Explain what Nelson Mandela meant when he said, "I either win or I learn."

_____

_____

FAILURE AND EMOTIONS

1. Is it better to try not to care about failure or to acknowledge that it hurts?

_____

_____

2. What happens when we try to pretend that failure doesn't hurt?

_____

_____

3. If we have an experience of failure but suppress our emotions about it instead of expressing and releasing them, what might happen the next time we find ourselves in a similar situation?

_____

_____

THE COURAGE TO MAKE MISTAKES, ESPECIALLY IN PUBLIC

1. Why does the idea of being wrong in public feel so scary to most people?

_____

_____

2. What are some advantages of being willing to make a mistake or be wrong in front of other people?

_____

_____

3. What can you do if you ask an honest question and someone calls it stupid?

_____

_____

4. If you wanted to try to figure out the answer to a question before asking someone, how could you do that?

_____

_____

5. What could happen if you didn't ask a question because you were afraid of being made fun of?

_____

_____

6. What's the worst thing that could happen to someone if they asked a question and someone else made fun of them?

_____

_____

7. What is the *best* thing that could happen if you started asking more questions?

_____

_____

HANDOUT 9.5   A Process for Dealing with Negative Feedback or Failure

Big feelings are nothing to be ashamed of. We've all been there. Believe that you can face tough feedback and come away stronger and more confident, ready to overcome bigger challenges. This handout will show you how.

1. GET YOUR EMOTIONS OUT

In a safe, private place, express your feelings about the disappointment or failure. Have a good cry, punch pillows, put on sad or angry music, or vent to a friend. Give yourself about a half hour for this step, or more if necessary. Be aware that if it's a big disappointment, the feelings may take several days to completely release, but as soon as you feel able, go ahead to step 2.

2. REMIND YOURSELF THAT YOU ARE NOT ALONE

Remember that everyone experiences the sting of failure, your favorite people included. (See the optional exercise at the end of this worksheet.)

3. MAKE YOURSELF COMFORTABLE BEFORE YOU FACE THE FEEDBACK

Go to a work space that feels comfortable. If you find music helpful, put on some music. Get some extra pillows if you want. Make yourself a cup of hot tea or cocoa.

Remind yourself that it might not be so bad. If there have been times in the past where you dreaded looking closely at negative feedback, but when you made yourself do it, it actually wasn't so bad, then consciously recall that experience.

If you feel a lot of resistance, you may want to make a deal with a family member or a friend like, "I'm going to look at this test I failed, while you look at the comments on your book report, and we'll check in with each other in one hour." Sometimes, a very successful friend of mine actually calls one of her friends but both of them mute their phones. Just knowing that someone is there gives her the boost she needs to face the feedback.

4. REVIEW THE FEEDBACK

Get out the test, essay, project, game film, or whatever it is. If it's a test, look at the questions you got wrong one by one. If it's an essay or a project, take each of your teacher's comments one by one. If you are reviewing a game or a performance, take the recording a few minutes at a time. Before you begin, take out two blank sheets of paper. At the top of one of them write *Lessons Learned*. At the top of the other, write *Questions*. (You can also use the sheets provided with this worksheet.)

For each piece of feedback:

1. See what went wrong.

2. If you understand your mistake and know how to correct it, then write that down on the *Lessons Learned* sheet.

3. If you don't understand your mistake, sit with it for a few minutes and see if you can work it out.

4. If you worked it out, make note of it on the *Lessons Learned* sheet.

5. If you weren't able to work it out, make note of it on the *Questions* sheet.

5. REWARD YOURSELF FOR FACING THE FEEDBACK

Choose a simple reward, perhaps an activity you enjoy, to congratulate yourself for facing your weaknesses. It is something that a lot of people struggle to do, and you deserve a big pat on the back for doing it.

6. GET YOUR QUESTIONS ANSWERED

Arrange a meeting with your teacher or the person who gave you the feedback. Begin the appointment by thanking the person for taking the time to give you feedback and letting them know that you went through all of it but had a few questions you'd like to discuss.

7. CHECK TO SEE IF IT WAS WORTH IT

A few weeks later, assess how much facing the feedback helped you. Doing this step should encourage you that there's a substantial reward for going through the discomfort of facing difficult feedback.

8. CONFIDENTLY FACE THE FUTURE

Now that you have used the negative feedback to improve, you know that's an option, and you won't be walking around with the idea that something is impossible. Think about whether you want to use the experience to go even deeper into the activity or to focus your efforts elsewhere.

Congratulations on turning an obstacle into a valuable learning experience!

Reviewing Feedback

LESSONS LEARNED:

_____

_____

_____

_____

_____

_____

_____

_____

_____

_____

_____

_____

_____

_____

_____

_____

_____

_____

Reviewing Feedback

QUESTIONS:

_____

_____

_____

_____

_____

_____

_____

_____

_____

_____

_____

_____

_____

_____

_____

_____

_____

_____

_____

_____

_____

_____

_____

OPTIONAL EXERCISE:

List three of the people you respect the most, who you think don't let failure get to them. These people could be celebrities—athletes, artists, scientists, businesspeople, or anyone in the public eye—or people you actually know. Search the internet for celebrities' worst failures or interview the people you know about their worst failure and how they overcame it. Whenever you are feeling down about something that didn't work out for you, remember that these people went through it too.

Name 1: _____

Failure: _____

Name 2: _____

Failure: _____

Name 3: _____

Failure: _____

HANDOUT 9.6   **Defining Success**

Success means different things to different people. One person might feel successful if they run their own business. Another might feel successful if they are a kind person who contributes to society. A third might find success in raising children. But the most important definition of success is your own. Keep in mind that your definition of success might change or evolve.

1. What do you think the typical definition of success is?

    _____

    _____

    _____

    _____

2. What do you think it means to be successful?

    _____

    _____

    _____

    _____

3. How can you remind yourself to act according to your own definition of success, rather than what other people might think?

    _____

    _____

    _____

    _____

HANDOUT 10.1 Study Preferences

The purpose of this worksheet is to spend some time thinking about what makes studying and learning more comfortable and enjoyable for you. Keep in mind, though, that even if conditions aren't ideal, your academic performance can still be stellar. Being aware of our needs and preferences helps us compensate and adjust when conditions aren't ideal for us.

For example, let's say you prefer sitting on a cushion when you work. So maybe you sit on your folded jacket when taking a test in class. Or, say your focus improves when you have an early afternoon snack. But one day you forget your snack, so you buy some trail mix from the vending machine. Or let's say you prefer bright lighting, but you need to work in a library that has dim fluorescent bulbs. You might take your study breaks outside in the sunshine.

The point is that the better you know yourself and what you prefer, the more you can get creative and come up with solutions when you don't have exactly what you want. Keep in mind that your preferences might stay the same for a long time, or change at any time. Check in with yourself and see what you need.

If you read some of the following questions and don't have any preferences one way or the other, try experimenting with the different options, and see what works best for you.

WHERE I LIKE TO STUDY

1. Here are all the places I enjoy doing schoolwork in my home: (Possible answers: bedroom, kitchen, living room, dining room, den, basement, other.)

   _____

   _____

2. Here are all the places I enjoy doing schoolwork outside my home: (Possible answers: particular libraries at school, public libraries, cafés, parks, other.)

   _____

   _____

HOW I LIKE MY STUDY ENVIRONMENT

3. Do I prefer complete silence or some background noise when I work? (If you have no preference, write that down.)

   _____

   _____

4. Do I find music distracting or helpful? (If your answer is "distracting," skip to question 5.)

_____

_____

    4b. Does it matter to me if the music has lyrics? _____

    4c. Does the type of music matter to me? If so, which styles or genres feel helpful? _____

_____

_____

HOW I WILL KEEP MYSELF FROM GETTING DISTRACTED

5. Here are all the devices I own: (Possible answers: computer, tablet, phone.)

_____

_____

6. For each device, here are the ways I will keep myself distraction-free while I study: (Possible answers: disable banner and sound notifications, put phone in airplane mode.)

_____

_____

7. Would it help me to track my screen time or app usage? Why or why not?

_____

_____

8. Would it help me to have a digital detox app or uninstall some apps on one or more of my devices? Why or why not?

_____

_____

HOW I LIKE TO KEEP MY BRAIN IN TIP-TOP SHAPE

9. Here are all the kinds of physical activity that I enjoy: (Possible answers: walking the dog, riding my bike, swimming, playing some sort of sport or game, hiking or walking in nature, taking dance classes, performing, playing video games with a physical component like dancing or miming sports, etc. It can be anything where you move. Feel free to just circle some of the options.)

    _____

    _____

10. Do I need to carry snacks to make sure I don't get too hungry or drained during the day?

    _____

11. How many hours of sleep makes me feel rested? _____

12. Why are downtime and rest important?

    _____

    _____

13. Why is sleep important?

    _____

    _____

HANDOUT 10.2 Study Session Checklist

The following is a checklist to make sure you have everything you need when it's time to learn. Feel free to cross out items or add items.

IT'S TIME TO LEARN! DO I HAVE:

☐ a comfortable workspace?

☐ the right sound environment for me?

☐ good lighting?

☐ devices and notifications muted or turned off?

☐ the conditions I need to concentrate?

☐ pencils and/or pens?

☐ study tools (for example, flashcards, highlighter pens, etc.)?

☐ the reading material I need?

☐ the notes, notebooks, or folders I need?

☐ extra paper?

☐ a timer?

☐ water?

☐ _____

☐ _____

☐ _____

☐ _____

HANDOUT 10.3   Rocks in a Bucket

If you have to fit sand, pebbles, water, and big rocks in a bucket, in which order would you place the four types of items in the bucket?

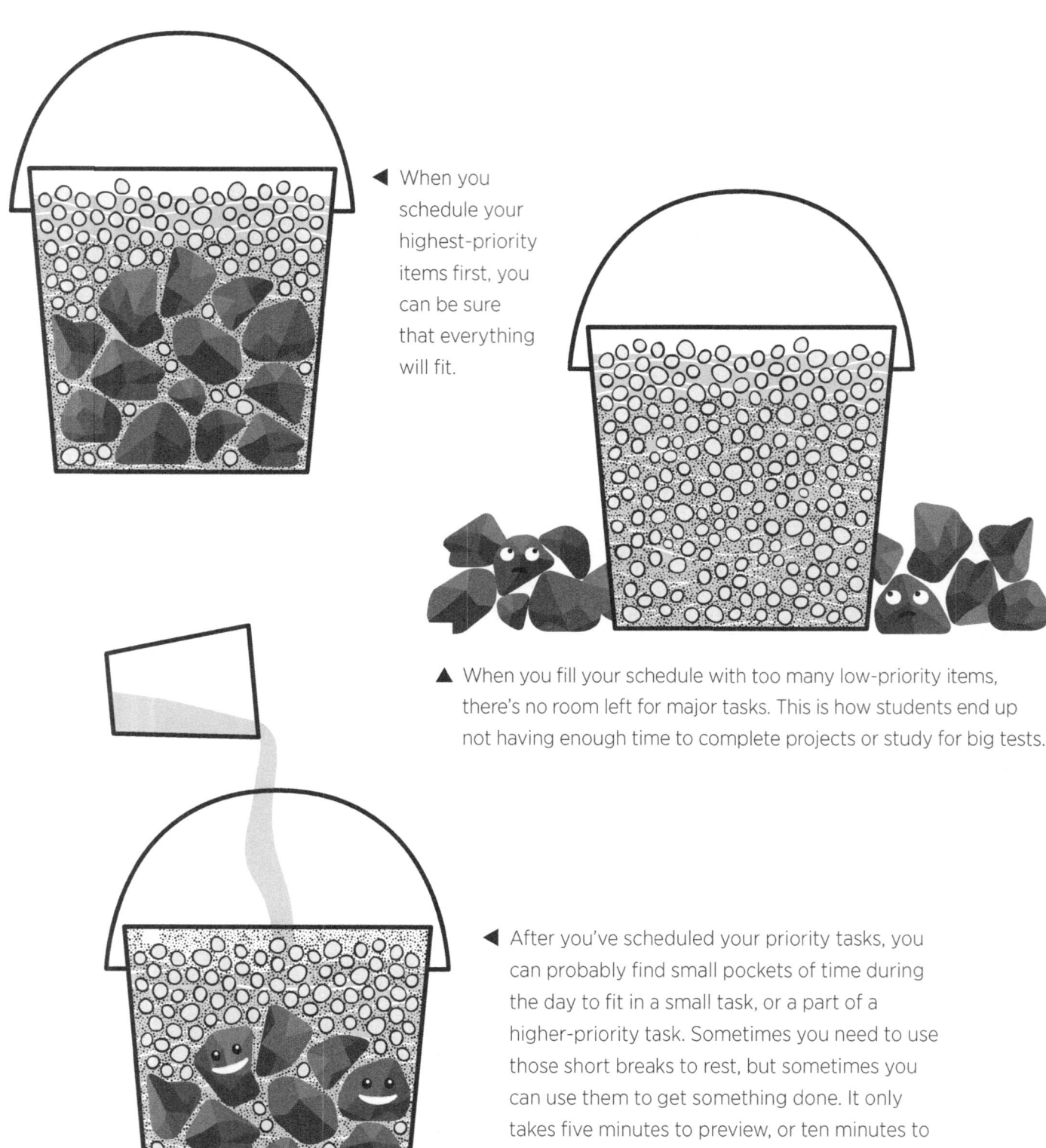

◄ When you schedule your highest-priority items first, you can be sure that everything will fit.

▲ When you fill your schedule with too many low-priority items, there's no room left for major tasks. This is how students end up not having enough time to complete projects or study for big tests.

◄ After you've scheduled your priority tasks, you can probably find small pockets of time during the day to fit in a small task, or a part of a higher-priority task. Sometimes you need to use those short breaks to rest, but sometimes you can use them to get something done. It only takes five minutes to preview, or ten minutes to do a homework problem.

There are several ways to create your Term Calendar. Here are a few:

1. You can create a physical Term Calendar by combining four or five Month Calendars (see page 3 of this handout).

2. You can purchase or download a current calendar for the year that you need it.

3. You can use an electronic calendar and fill in several months at a time to create an electronic Term Calendar.

To fill out your Term Calendar, you'll need to have the dates of major tests and projects for each of your classes Often, that information is found on the class syllabus. If your teachers do not provide a syllabus, then use any materials given to you in class, online class calendars, or other available scheduling information to fill out your calendar. As soon as new dates are posted or announced, you can add them to your Term Calendar. You'll also use information from all of your clubs, teams, performance groups, and other activities to fill it in. Your Term Calendar should show:

- all test dates

- all quiz dates

- due dates for all major projects

- due dates for all major papers

- dates for all field trips and other events

- dates of all games or performances

- dates of social events you are planning to attend, such as birthdays or other family gatherings

How to Use a Syllabus to Fill Out Your Term Calendar

WHY SHOULD I CARE ABOUT A SYLLABUS?

Many students just shove the syllabus they get from their teacher in their bag and never really read it because the information won't be relevant for weeks or months. But a syllabus has a ton of valuable information that will help you succeed and also enjoy the class more.

All of your class syllabi are important for time management because they tell you the tasks and dates that need to be scheduled on your calendar. They also often give you important information about how you should do your assignments and also how to find your teacher outside of class to ask questions or ask for help.

USING A SYLLABUS TO FILL OUT YOUR TERM CALENDAR

1. Use a highlighter and go through each page of your class syllabus, highlighting due dates. If your syllabus is electronic, use online highlighting options or make notes on a separate piece of paper (or in a digital document).

2. Enter into your calendar each of these due dates with a short description of what's due. (Examples: "Bonding quiz," "Unit 3 test," "Term paper on the Dark Ages," "Genetics lab report," "Algebra II Final")

3. Get the syllabus for your next class and repeat steps above.

Once you've done this for all of your syllabi, your Term Calendar will be complete. If you notice that it seems too full, start thinking about what you may want to cut back on, and present a convincing case for your choices to your parents.

TERM CALENDAR

	SUNDAY	MONDAY	TUESDAY	WEDNESDAY	THURSDAY	FRIDAY	SATURDAY
MONTH/YEAR:							

	SUNDAY	MONDAY	TUESDAY	WEDNESDAY	THURSDAY	FRIDAY	SATURDAY
MONTH/YEAR:							

	SUNDAY	MONDAY	TUESDAY	WEDNESDAY	THURSDAY	FRIDAY	SATURDAY
MONTH/YEAR:							

HANDOUT 10.5   Filling Out Your Weekly Calendar

There are several ways to create your Weekly Calendars. Here are a few:

1. You can create a physical Weekly Calendar by printing out the calendar on page 2 of this handout.

2. You can purchase or download a current calendar or planner for the year.

3. You can use an electronic calendar and fill it in a week at a time.

Fill in your Weekly Calendar with:

- all relevant items from your Term Calendar

- free periods at school

- work hours

- all after-school activities such as clubs, teams, lessons, rehearsals, practices

- study time

- socializing time

- sleep (aim for at least 7 hours per night)

Get in the habit of filling in your weekly calendar on the weekend when you have some downtime. If you notice that your calendar is getting uncomfortably full, think about what you can cut or push to a later time so that you're set up to have an enjoyable week.

Get in the habit of starting a homework assignment as soon as you get it. Following this guideline gives you the best shot at finishing your assignments on time in a relaxed way. It also helps you identify gaps in your understanding early so that you have enough time to get help from your teacher or someone else before you have to take a quiz or test. It's easier to keep up than to catch up. So stay ahead of the game!

WEEKLY CALENDAR

	SUNDAY	MONDAY	TUESDAY	WEDNESDAY	THURSDAY	FRIDAY	SATURDAY
6:00 am							
7:00 am							
8:00 am							
9:00 am							
10:00 am							
11:00 am							
12:00 pm							
1:00 pm							
2:00 pm							
3:00 pm							
4:00 pm							
5:00 pm							
6:00 pm							
7:00 pm							
8:00 pm							
9:00 pm							
10:00 pm							
11:00 pm							
12:00 am							

HANDOUT 10.6   App Detox

If you want to change the amount of time you spend on your phone, tablet, or computer, try this strategy. When my grandson was a senior in high school, he used it to pull his Cs and Ds up to As and Bs.

STEP 1: List all of the apps on your phone, tablet, or computer that you would like to spend less time using.

App	Approximate time spent per day or week
TikTok	_____
Snapchat	_____
Instagram	_____
Twitter	_____
YouTube	_____
Twitch	_____
Facebook	_____
Discord	_____
_____	_____
_____	_____
_____	_____
_____	_____
_____	_____

STEP 2: List the apps in order of highest to lowest usage. There might already be a built-in app on your phone tracking this information. If not, you can just guess for now and then find an app later that will keep track of your screen time and app usage.

Apps listed in order of highest to lowest usage

1. _____

2. _____

3. _____

4. _____

5. _____

6. _____

7. _____

8. _____

9. _____

10. _____

11. _____

12. _____

13. _____

14. _____

15. _____

STEP 3: Uninstall and remove *all* of the apps from all of your devices and get your grades high enough to meet the minimum expectation of your parent or mentor, or high enough to meet your own minimum expectation, whichever is higher. This step will take the most time and energy.

STEP 4: Add back the last app on the list, the one you used the least. Wait three days to see if you start using it too much.

STEP 5: If your work habits have gotten lax, remove the app again. But if you've been able to keep up with your schoolwork, add the next app on the list, and wait three more days.

STEP 6: Repeat step 5 until all your apps have been added back or until you've decided to quit some of them for good.

HANDOUT 10.7　Quiz: Saying No, Setting Boundaries, and Protecting Your Time

1. Your friend wants you to go to a party, but you don't actually want to go. They try begging and guilt-tripping you. You:

   a. Give in and go to the party. Your friend has been there for you in the past and you feel like you owe them.

   b. Tell your friend you're not going to the party but ask if they want to join you another time doing something that you know you would both enjoy.

   c. Tell your friend you're offended by their tactics and good luck at the party.

2. Your friend wants to study with you, but you don't find it that helpful to study with them. You:

   a. Study with them anyway because you feel like if anyone asks you for help, you should give it to them.

   b. Explain that you find it more helpful to study by yourself but offer them a half hour of your time to help them, whenever it is convenient for both of you.

   c. Tell them they drag you down and hold you back.

3. It's time for dinner, and your parent has called you to the table, but you're in the zone with a tricky project and can tell you'll need the rest of the evening to finish it. You:

   a. Stop working right away and go down for dinner.

   b. Say respectfully that you'll be there in a few minutes, jot down some notes so you can pick up your train of thought later, ask your parent if you can be excused earlier than normal to finish your assignment, calmly eat your dinner, and then return to your project.

   c. Yell out, "Stop bothering me! Can't you see I'm working here?!"

4. It's time to pick projects in class, but none of the suggested options appeal to you. You:

   a. Choose the one you hate the least, and just grit your teeth and resign yourself to doing it.

   b. Notice there's an option to pick your own topic and decide to take it. Even though you'll have to think a little harder about what to do, you know you'll enjoy it more than one of the suggested topics.

   c. Silently protest the whole stupid assignment by doing a terrible job.

5. Your younger sibling wants to play with you during a time you had set aside for studying. You:

   a. Put down your pencil and go play so that you won't get terrorized with a tantrum.

   b. Explain that you can't right now, but you'll have 15 minutes in about an hour to play.

   c. Slam the door and tell them to stop bothering you.

6. There's a legitimate crisis in the group chat, but you only have two hours to finish a big project that will count for a third of your grade. You:

    a. Drop everything because a friend is in crisis. Spend an hour offering comfort and advice, and accept that you'll just get a lower grade in that class.

    b. Get to the end of your Focused Study Session. Set a timer for ten minutes. Spend the first five minutes getting caught up on the drama, and then reply with something like, "I'm so sorry this is happening to you. Sending so much love and support, and we'll definitely talk about it tomorrow when I see you. I wish I could stay longer, but I gotta finish this thing." The next day at school, you spend most of your break time with your friend.

    c. Ignore the chat entirely.

7. Someone you think is cute wants to meet on Twitch, but you're only halfway through your planned reading. You:

    a. Think to yourself, "When will I ever have this opportunity again?" and start gaming with them.

    b. Write back something like, "Ugh, still working. What are you doing in two hours? Or tomorrow?" You'll know that if they're not still interested then, they were never really interested in the first place.

    c. Block them.

8. YouTube suggests a video from one of your favorite accounts while you're deep in thought studying for a big test. You:

    a. Click on it immediately, reasoning that it'll only be a few minutes.

    b. Close the notification and take the opportunity to turn off all notifications. Finish what you're doing, and watch a few minutes of the video on your next break.

    c. Uninstall YouTube.

9. You have the option of taking a class about a subject you love or one that you think someone else in your life wants you to take. You:

    a. Sign up for the class that will get you someone else's approval. The discomfort of that confrontation isn't worth it to you.

    b. Take a deep breath and decide to be honest with the person about what you want to do. The worst they can do is tell you no and put pressure on you to make another choice. You can handle that and keep asking for what you want.

    c. Secretly sign up for the class you want to take but lie and say that you signed up for the other one.

10. There's a big concert you want to go to the night before an extremely important test, and your parents don't want you to go. You:

   a. Don't go.

   b. Figure out how to schedule your study time so that you're ready to ace the test on the day after the concert. You present your plan to your parents and accept their final decision.

   c. Go and don't care if you fail the test.

Count the number of As, Bs, and Cs that you answered. See the next page to interpret your results.

Number of As: _____

Number of Bs: _____

Number of Cs: _____

QUIZ SCORING KEY:

If you answered mostly As:

It seems like you really care about others, sometimes at the expense of taking care of yourself. See if you can find the courage to speak up and be willing to have disagreements with others so that you can find compromises that work for you and the other person. There's nothing wrong with having a disagreement, as long as it stays civil, and there's also nothing wrong with fighting for something you want and not getting it in the end. The more you ask for what you want, the more you may hear "no," but you will also hear more "yes." The end result is that you have more of what you want in your life. Remember, athletes who make more shots also *take* more shots and miss more shots. So be courageous. Speak up. You only have one life. Spend your time doing the things you care about the most.

If you answered mostly Bs:

Congratulations! You have excellent boundaries and are skilled at finding compromises between what you want to do and what others want you to do. Continue advocating for yourself and being kind to others.

If you answered mostly Cs:

You have a very strong sense of what you need and want. Continue protecting your time, but make sure not to be too curt with others. Social skills are important for doing well in school and in life.

The purpose of this worksheet is to help you identify what you think is important and what you might want to do in the future so that you can connect your schoolwork to what you want to do in life.

You may or may not already know what you want to do in adulthood. Some people know what they want to do from the time they are three years old, and other people are well into their twenties before they choose a path. One is no better than the other.

The point of expressing your values, goals, and dreams is *not* to make a decision that you feel you have to stick with for the rest of your life. What we want can change. The point of this activity is for you to express what you find important *right now* and to explore how your schoolwork connects to those things.

- **Part I of this activity is identifying some things that may be important to you: values, goals, and dreams.**

- **Part II of this activity is visualizing your future self in various circumstances.**

- **Part III of this activity is making a board, poster, booklet, or other concrete reminder of what you'll discover today.**

I recommend doing all three, but if you're short on time, just do Part I.

PART I: What do you feel strongly about?

VALUES

Please look at this list of values and circle any and all that speak to you. There is space at the end to write down anything that you don't find on this list.

Achievement, Adventure, Autonomy, Balance, Challenge, Community, Competency, Contribution, Creativity, Fairness, Faith, Family, Friendships, Fun, Growth, Honesty, Humor, Inner Harmony, Innovation, Kindness, Knowledge, Leadership, Optimism, Peace, Popularity, Recognition, Respect, Responsibility, Security, Self-Respect, Service, Success, Trustworthiness, Wealth, Wisdom, _____

_____

GOALS

Circle or write down *any and all* of these possible professional goals that interest you.

- Run a business. If so, what kind(s) _____

- Master an art or a skill. If so, which one(s) _____

- (Any skill in any of the performing or visual arts, writing, athletics, cooking, designing/tailoring, being any kind of stylist, tradesperson, craftsperson, architect, builder, graphic designer, or computer programmer are just some of the options that could go here.)

- Become a doctor, nurse, physical therapist, psychologist, or other healing professional.

- Become a lawyer, judge, or other law professional.

- Become a teacher, professor, or other education professional.

- Become a politician.

- Become a scientist or tech-industry professional.

- Become a journalist or other media professional.

- Become an independent consultant, coach, trainer, or other paid advisor to others.

- Become a priest, pastor, or other theological professional.

- Have a family.

- Work for a nonprofit or work for social, environmental, political (etc.) change.

- Become a farmer or someone who works in agriculture.

- Join the military, law enforcement, or emergency services.

- Other _____

_____

Possible goals after high school and beyond

- Attend a particular college, conservatory, or technical school. If so, which one(s) _____

_____

_____

_____

- Spend some time abroad. If so, where? _____

- Participate in a volunteer service program, either abroad or in your home country. _____

_____

- Live in a particular place. If so, where? _____

- Own a house, condo, or car. If so, describe what you want _____

- Other _____

_____

_____

_____

DREAMS

If you could do absolutely anything you wanted to do, what would it be? Write three things down if you can, but one is good too.

1. _____

2. _____

3. _____

Now look over everything you've just written down and **list the top five things from all of the sections that you feel the most strongly about**. You could list all values, all goals, all dreams, or any combination of the three. The sample answer shows a combination, but you can choose five of the same type of thing if you want to. Just list the top five things that make your insides feel like they're smiling the most. You will use this list during the activity on Handout 11.2.

Sample Answer:

1. *community* (value)

2. *getting an internship at the Gazette* (goal)

3. *playing professional baseball* (dream)

4. *living in Ghana* (dream)

5. *being a top editor at a regional newspaper* (goal)

1. _____

2. _____

3. _____

4. _____

5. _____

PART II: Imagine the Future

For this exercise you need a comfortable place to sit or lie down and a timer.

- Set your timer for five or ten minutes.

- Spend about a minute just relaxing and taking deep, slow breaths. Get comfortable.

- Then call to mind just one of your dreams, goals, or values.

- As you continue to breathe deeply and slowly, imagine your life while you are living out your dream, goal, or value. Add as much detail as you want to. Your imagination might be highly visual and you might see all sorts of pictures, or you might mostly imagine how things will make you *feel*, or maybe you will imagine lots of sounds or tastes. It's completely up to you. The idea is to have fun imagining doing something in life that excites you. And it doesn't have to be fancy or dramatic. It can be sitting on a beach or a park bench, enjoying the sunset.

- When the timer goes off, open your eyes.

- If it feels right, write down some details of what you imagined. If not, take one more deep breath and go on with your day.

Whenever you are struggling with some schoolwork or you're frustrated because you need to learn something that feels completely irrelevant to your life, you can close your eyes, breathe deeply, and return to what you saw, heard, felt, or tasted during your imagining. And you can remind yourself that what you are trying to learn is actually connected, no matter how indirectly, to that life of enjoyment and fulfillment.

PART III: Vision Boarding—Giving Yourself Concrete Reminders of What You Want

The purpose of this exercise is to give yourself something to regularly look at that reminds you why you want to engage deeply with your schoolwork. You can do this exercise with mostly digital resources and have the final product as a digital image or short movie. Or you can do it with paper materials, like print editions of newspapers and magazines, and your final product can be a poster, corkboard, or journal.

STEP 1:

Decide which things from your goals and dreams you want to put on your vision board. It can be very focused or very broad. One student might have everything that has to do with jazz trumpeting on the board and nothing else. Another might have images from many different countries, professions, and hobbies. It's totally up to you.

STEP 2:

Cut relevant text and images out from magazines, websites, newspapers. Find stock photos on the internet or take your own photos. Make your own drawings if you want. If you're making a video, find relevant clips.

STEP 3:

Get yourself a piece of poster board, a corkboard, several pieces of paper that you can t e together in a booklet, or a large journal with blank pages. Arrange all the pieces of your vision in whatever way you want. If you're working digitally, edit your image or video.

STEP 4:

Put your vision someplace where you can regularly look at it as a reminder of what is fueling your efforts.

When you're in the middle of a class that you m ght hate and everything is going terribly, you can call to mird your vision as a reminder about why it's important to learn something that you can't see any point of right in that moment. You can take a deep breath and think to yourself, "OK, this is worth learning properly because it will help me get to where I want to go."

HANDOUT 11.2 Mapping Out Your Year

The purpose of this activity is to help you think of schoolwork primarily as a tool for learning and *getting what you want in life*.

First, list the learning strategies and study tools you want to use for most of your classes. Then use your answers from Handout 11.1 to fill out the chart on the next page and connect your schoolwork to your goals and values.

The learning strategies I will definitely use in most of my classes are:

The reading strategies (Strategies #1 – 4). The teaching strategy (Strategy #5).

The Study Cycle (Strategy #9).

The study tools I will definitely use in most of my classes are:

Notetaking or Mapping.

I have partially filled in your answers on this page because *everyone* should be using the reading and teaching strategies, as well as The Study Cycle. You may have additional strategies and tools to fill in on this page, but it's okay if you don't.

CLASS NAME	GOAL OR VALUE	BLOOM'S LEVEL REQ'D	EXTRA STRATEGIES?	EXTRA TOOLS?	HELP OPTIONS
AP Government	Work at a food insecurity nonprofit	4 or 5	Homework strategy	Flashcards, timelines	Mr. Dunwoody, Big Sis
Algebra	Get into U of M	3 or 4	Homework strategy	Graphing	Mrs. Miller, Afterschool tutors

HANDOUT 11.2 ▪ PAGE 2 OF 2

HANDOUT 11.3   Getting the Most Out of a Syllabus

STEP 1:

Choose one of your classes. Write out all of the questions you can think of about that class. Some examples: How many tests are there? What about projects or term papers? How will I be graded? How will the homework assignments affect my grade? How does my teacher want to be contacted? Any question you are curious about, write it down.

_____

_____

_____

_____

_____

_____

_____

_____

_____

_____

_____

_____

_____

_____

STEP 2:

Now read the syllabus and find the answers to your questions. If you don't have a syllabus, use your class notes, online calendars, and other available information to answer the questions. List the answers here.

_____

_____

_____

_____

_____

_____

_____

_____

_____

_____

_____

_____

STEP 3:

If there are some answers you couldn't find, see if your parent or mentor can help you find those.

STEP 4:

If you still have questions after Step 3, then go see your teacher. Begin that meeting by explaining that you read the syllabus carefully or looked for all of the information you could find. Say that you found answers to many of your questions, but you had some that you couldn't answer. That way, you show respect for your teacher's time and you also get your questions answered.

Follow this procedure for all of your classes.

HANDOUT 11.4   Procrastination Busters

Here are seven of the most powerful ways I know of to stop putting things off. I hope you find them useful. Number 3, about timers, is especially useful.

1. THE TWO-QUESTION TECHNIQUE

Ask yourself:

1. What do I need to do?

2. What is the barrier to doing it?

2. BREAK IT DOWN

Break whatever you are doing down into smaller steps. If those steps need to be broken down into even smaller steps, then do that. If *those* steps need to be broken down further, then do that. This technique is discussed extensively in Handout 8.4: How to Figure Out What You Are Actually Supposed to Be Doing.

3. USE A TIMER AND DO A FOCUSED STUDY SESSION

Timers are very popular and powerful tools for boosting productivity. When you use a timer, you always know a break is coming soon. Timers are great to use for Focused Study Sessions or just to get 10 or 20 minutes of work done here or there.

Every cellphone has a timer, but make sure that the phone itself is not a distraction. Put it in airplane mode or make sure all your notifications are disabled. If the phone is still too distracting, then **ask your parent or mentor to get you a stand-alone timer, such as a digital kitchen timer**.

But if you *can* handle using timers on your digital devices, then there are lots of great online timers and apps, such as tomato-timer.com. When you put limits on both work time and break time, just as you are directed to do during Focused Study Sessions, then you can always stay on track.

4. 10 MINUTES ON, 10 MINUTES OFF

Sometimes a task just feels so daunting that working on it for even 15 minutes seems like torture. In that case, you might be able to lure yourself to the task by promising yourself a whole 10 minutes of break time after just 10 minutes of work time. (One of the most productive people I know, when she *reallly* doesn't want to do something, does 5 minutes on, 5 minutes off. One time she even did 1 minute on, 10 minutes off.)

You could say that this technique turns a 1-hour task into a 2-hour task, but usually, what it *actually* does is make sure you finish something in 2 hours instead of having your energy eaten up for 3 days thinking and worrying about it.

What usually happens is that the "on" periods start to stretch into longer blocks of time as you get into the task and find your groove.

5. COUNTDOWNS

When you're in the middle of a reading assignment that just feels like it's never going to end, you can count the number of sections left. After you finish each section, you think to yourself, "Only 3 sections left" or "Only 6 sections left." Just knowing that number is getting smaller can give you the energy to keep going and finish.

6. BUDDY UP

With this strategy, you text a friend and each agree to do something you're putting off. Agree to check in with each other to confirm you did it. Buddying up in this way should not take more than one minute per check-in. For example, you could text "Need to read chapter 5" and then "Did it" after you finished. That would take you less than 30 seconds total. If you are texting with your phone, then after each text, immediately put it back in airplane mode.

7. GIVE YOURSELF CONSEQUENCES

Whenever I really need to do something I keep putting off, I promise to give one of my children $100 if I don't do it. Sure enough, I get it done! Consider promising one of your parents that you'll do extra chores or one of your siblings that you'll do something that they enjoy and you don't. But the idea behind consequences should be playful and lighthearted. We're not trying to punish ourselves. We always deserve kindness.

HANDOUT 11.5 Exam Wrappers

You can use this technique* every time a test is returned to you. It will help you make useful changes to your preparation process. If they haven't done so already, your parent or mentor will download or give you a copy of the Test Preparation Guide so that you can discover the best way to prepare for tests, as well as useful tips for test day. The Guide also tells you what to do if your teacher doesn't return tests.

If you were really disappointed with your grade and feel unable to face this process, have a look at Handout 9.5: A Process for Dealing with Negative Feedback or Failure for some ideas about how to feel better and find the courage you need.

STEP 1:

Ask yourself, "What worked? Which study strategies and tools were effective?"

_____

_____

_____

_____

_____

STEP 2:

Ask yourself, "What didn't work?"

Did you need more time to prepare? Did you focus on some topics too much or not enough on others? Did you need a different study tool? Or some extra help from your teacher? Were there specific skills, like writing a good essay or doing a certain kind of math proof, that you weren't able to master in time? Ask yourself as many questions about your preparation process as you can think of, and list everything you think you could have improved.

_____

_____

_____

_____

_____

*A learning strategist named Marsha Lovett at Carnegie Mellon University created this technique.

STEP 3:

Ask yourself, "What will I do differently next time?"

Look at every item you wrote down for step 2. Now decide what changes you want to make to each one in order to do better on your next test.

_____

_____

_____

_____

_____

_____

_____

_____

HANDOUT 11.6   Learning Strategies Inventory

This inventory lists the things that you should do if you want to do well in a class. Write "true" or "false" beside each of the following statements describing the way you study. The scoring scale at the end will predict your grade in the class.

1. I always preview the material that will be discussed before I go to class.

2. I go over my class notes as soon as possible after class to rework them and note problem areas.

3. I try to do my homework without using example problems as a guide or copying answers from my class notes or textbook.

4. I regularly seek help to discuss problems or questions about the homework.

5. Before each test, I rework all the homework problems and quiz questions that I previously had trouble with.

6. I spend some time studying for this class at least five days per week (outside of class).

7. I use flashcards or other study tools to help me remember facts and equations.

8. I make diagrams or draw mental pictures of the concepts discussed in class.

9. I participate in a study group, where we do homework and quiz ourselves on the material.

10. I rework all of the quiz and test items I missed *before* the next class session.

11. I realize that I can still do well in this class even if I have done poorly on the quizzes and tests up to this point.

Here is the predicted grade for your performance in this class:

NUMBER OF TRUE RESPONSES	PREDICTED GRADE
9 or more	A
6–8	B
4–5	C
2–3	D
less than 2	F

Note that you can change your predicted grade *at any point* by changing your behavior to make more of these statements true.

HANDOUT 11.7   Strategies and Tools Tracker

Use this table to keep track of which strategies and tools are working well for you. You will rate the effectiveness of each strategy or tool from 1 to 5. An example appears on the next page, and a table for you to fill in appears on the page after that. You can update this table whenever you want. Doing it once a month is a great idea, or you could do one class per week. Here's the ratings system you'll use:

1 = didn't work at all

2 = worked okay

3 = much better than not doing anything

4 = got me the results I wanted

5 = made me do even better than I expected

STRATEGIES AND TOOLS TRACKER

CLASS	STRATEGY OR TOOL	EFFECTIVENESS ON A SCALE 1-5	SOMETHING NEW TO TRY
Algebra I	Flashcards	3	More time on homework strategy
	Reading strategies	5	—
History	Teaching strategy	4	Do it more often
	Reading strategies with note-taking	4	Try mind mapping
English	Flashcards	4	Review on the bus to school
	Homework strategy	2	Go see Ms. Lopez to improve my essays
Biology	Mnemonic devices	5	
	Teaching strategy	3	Do the homework strategy too
	Using the textbook	3	Remember to preview

STRATEGIES AND TOOLS TRACKER

CLASS	STRATEGY OR TOOL	EFFECTIVENESS ON A SCALE 1-5	SOMETHING NEW TO TRY

HANDOUT 11.8   When Overwhelm Strikes

Use this procedure when you feel overwhelmed by the number of strategies, tools, and assignments to choose from or by the number of decisions to make. Even though it may not feel like it, doing *something* is usually better than doing nothing. One exception is when you really need to sleep or rest. At those times, sleeping and resting are just as productive as working.

STEP 1:

Choose **one** strategy. It can be anything, but I suggest the teaching strategy.

STEP 2:

Choose **one** tool. It can be anything, but I suggest note-taking *or* making mind maps, charts, tables, or timelines.

STEP 3:

Sit down for a 30-minute Focused Study Session.

- Plan for 1 minute

- Study for 20 minutes

- Break for 4 minutes

- Recap for 5 minutes

Return to step 1.

HANDOUT 11.9   Quick Reference List of All Learning Support Resources

I strongly recommend having the following handouts read ly available, in a booklet or folder, throughout the school year. You have several options:

1. Carefully detach the pages from this book and place most of them in a folder and some of them on a corkboard, where you can see them.

2. Simply bookmark pages in this book with brightly colored post-its or sticky page markers (sometimes called flags).

3. Ask your parent, guardian, or mentor to print copies from www.studyandlearn.guide/resources-content, or show you how to do so. Then place most of them in a folder and some of them on a corkboard, where you can see them.

ESSENTIAL RESOURCES

- 4.5: Bloom's Levels of Learning
- 5.3: Study Cycle with Focused Study Sessions
- 6.3: Ten Learning Strategies
- 6.5: Quick Reference: List of Study Tools
- 7.1: Fixed and Growth Mindsets
- 8.4: How to Figure Out What You Are Actually Supposed to Be Doing
- 11.2: Mapping Out Your Year
- 11.3: Getting the Most Out of a Syllabus
- 11.5: Exam Wrappers
- 11.8: When Overwhelm Strikes
- Appendix A: Test Preparation Guide

The following list includes several resources you may find extremely useful to keep in your booklet or folder:

RECOMMENDED RESOURCES

- Appendix B: Study Tools Guide
- 8.3: How Do You Prefer to Learn?
- 8.5: Self-Talk Journaling Worksheet
- 9.5: A Procedure for Dealing with Negative Feedback or Failure
- 10.2: Study Session Checklist
- 10.4: Filling Out Your Term Calendar
- 10.5: Filling Out Your Weekly Calendar
- 11.4: Procrastination Busters

Handouts 12.1 and 12.2 lay out a framework for leading students through the learning strategies, study techniques, and motivational exercises given in *The Parents' Guide*. The page numbers in the table correspond to page numbers in *The Parents' Guide*, in which I give a step-by-step explanation for choosing what material to present and how to present it. Keep in mind that the pacing with which you go through the material is up to you, depending on what works for your family.

Although the location of the handouts is given as "web" in the tables, you can of course find them in this book of handouts. (Page numbers of the handouts are not given in the tables so as not to confuse *The Parents' Guide* page numbers with *Handouts* page numbers. The sequential ordering of the handouts in this book should make it easy to find them.)

HANDOUT 12.1   Core Content

CORE CONTENT (with *Parents' Guide* page references as well as time frame suggestions per chapter)

RESOURCE	LOCATION	TITLE	TIME (EST)
Chapter 3		**Metacognition**	10–20 mins
Ch 3 Script	pp. 25–28	—	
Ch 3 Script Summary	29	—	
Handout 3.1	web*	Who is Dr. McGuire and Why Should I Care About What She Says?	
Handout 3.2	web	What is Metacognition and How Can It Help Me?	
Handout 3.3	web	Count the Vowels	
Handout 3.4	web	Metacognition Worksheet	
Answer Key 3.4A	31–33	Answer Key for Metacognition Worksheet	
Chapter 4		**Bloom's Levels Of Learning**	15–20 mins
Ch 4 Script	35–38	—	
Ch 4 Script Summary	39	—	
Handout 4.1	web	Answering Reflection Questions	
Handout 4.2	web	Other Students' Answers to Reflection Question #1	
Handout 4.3	web	Other Students' Answers to Reflection Question #3	
Handout 4.4	web	Alternative Answers to Reflection Question #3	
Handout 4.5	web	Bloom's Levels of Learning	
Handout 4.6	web	Bloom's Levels of Learning: Goldilocks Edition	
Answer Key 4.6A	43	Answer Key for Bloom's Levels of Learning: Goldilocks Edition	
Chapter 5		**The Study Cycle**	5–10 mins
Ch 5 Script	46–48	—	
Ch 5 Script Summary	49–50	—	
Handout 5.1	web	The Study Cycle	
Handout 5.2	web	Focused Study Sessions	
Handout 5.3	web	The Study Cycle and Focused Study Sessions Combined	
Chapter 6		**Ten Learning Strategies**	30–35 mins
Ch 6 Script	56–62	—	
Ch 6 Script Summary	64–66	—	
Handout 6.1	web	Guess the Activity/The Power of Previewing	
Handout 6.2	web	Using Your Homework to Test Your Understanding	
Handout 6.3	web	Ten Learning Strategies	

*Although the location of the handouts is given as "web" in the tables, you can of course find them in this book of handouts in their sequential ordering.   *(continued)*

Core Content (continued)

RESOURCE	LOCATION	TITLE	TIME (EST.)
Handout 6.4	web*	Learning Strategies Worksheet	
Handout 6.5	web	Quick Reference: List of Study Tools	
Chapter 7		**Mindset**	**20–25 mins**
Ch 7 Script	72–76	—	
Ch 7 Script Summary	77–78	—	
Handout 7.1	web	Fixed and Growth Mindsets	
Handout 7.2	web	Mindset Worksheet	
Answer Key 7.2A	82	Answer Key for Select Questions on Mindset Worksheet	
Chapter 8		**Motivation**	**25 mins**
Ch 8 Handout Roundup	102–103	—	
Handout 8.2	web	Worksheet about My Interests and Things I Enjoy Doing	
Handout 8.3	web	How Do You Prefer to Learn? (Worksheet)	
Handout 8.4	web	How to Figure Out What You Are Actually Supposed to Be Doing	
Chapter 9		**Dealing With Failure**	**15–25 mins**
Ch 9 Handout Roundup	117–118	—	
Handout 9.2	web	Dealing with Setbacks, Mistakes, and Failure	
Handout 9.4	web	Mistakes and Failure Worksheet	
Answer Key 9.4A	122–123	Answer Key for Mistakes and Failure Worksheet	
Chapter 10		**Planning And Time Management**	**15–30 mins**
Ch 10 Handout Roundup	132–133	—	
Handout 10.1	web	Study Preferences Worksheet	
Handout 10.3	web	Rocks in a Bucket	
Handout 10.4	web	Filling Out Your Term Calendar	
Handout 10.5	web	Filling Out Your Weekly Calendar	
Chapter 11		**Action Roundup For Students**	**15–30 mins**
Ch 11 Handout Roundup	135–139	—	
Handout 11.1	web	What Gets You Fired Up Deep Down Inside? PART I ONLY	
Handout 11.2	web	Mapping Out Your Year	
Handout 11.3	web	Getting the Most Out of a Syllabus	
Handout 11.5	web	Exam Wrappers	
Handout 11.8	web	When Overwhelm Strikes	
Handout 11.9	web	Quick Reference List of All Learning Support Resources	
Appendix A	web	Test Preparation Guide	

* Although the location of the handouts is given as "web" in the tables, you can of course find them in this book of handouts in their sequential ordering.

ADDITIONAL CONTENT (with *Parents' Guide* page references as well as time frame suggestions per handout)

RESOURCE	LOCATION	TITLE	TIME (EST.)
Chapter 8		**Motivation**	
Ch 8 Handout Roundup	pp. 102–103	—	
Handout 8.5	web*	Self-Talk Journaling Worksheet	**5–10 mins**
Handout 8.6	web	Doing What *You* Can and Letting Go of the Rest	**10–20 mins**
Chapter 9		**Dealing With Failure**	
Ch 9 Handout Roundup	117–118	—	
Handout 9.3	web	Stumbling Blocks or Stepping Stones?	**5 mins**
Handout 9.5	web	A Process for Dealing with Negative Feedback or Failure	**10 mins to introduce**
Handout 9.6	web	Worksheet—Defining Success	**(5–10 mins**
Chapter 10		**Planning and Time Management**	
Ch 10 Handout Roundup	132–133	—	
Handout 10.2	web	Study Session Checklist	**1–5 mins**
Handout 10.6	web	App Detox Worksheet	**5–10 mins to introduce**
Handout 10.7	web	Quiz: Saying No, Setting Boundaries, and Protecting Your Time	**5–15 mins**
Chapter 11		**Action Roundup for Students**	
Chapter 11 Handout Roundup	135–138	—	
Handout 11.1	web	What Gets You Fired Up Deep Down Inside? PARTS II and II	**20 mins or more**
Handout 11.4	web	Procrastination Busters	**5–10 mins**
Handout 11.6	web	Learning Strategies Inventory	**2–5 mins to introduce**
Handout 11.7	web	Strategies and Tools Tracker	**2–5 mins to introduce**
Appendix B			
Appendix B	web	Study Tools Guide	

* Although the location of the handouts is given as "web" in the tables, you can of course find them in this book of handouts in their sequential ordering.

Test Preparation Guide

Testing Tips

Before the test

1. Use the learning strategies in Chapter 6 and do homework as soon as it is assigned.

2. Find out what types of questions will be on the test and practice those types of questions. If you know you might have to write an essay about the events that started World War I, practice writing that essay. If you know you could be asked to solve four different types of trigonometry proofs, spend time mastering each type.

3. Prepare a study guide by organizing the information you need to master into charts, tables, outlines, timelines, or mind maps. If you want more information, see #5 of Appendix B: Study Tools Guide.

4. Set aside time slots to prepare for your test. Practice doing the questions or problems as quickly as you will be expected to do them during the test. If you typically run out of time on tests, figure out about how much time you will have for the different kinds of questions or problems. If you have trouble, talk to your teacher. Then use a timer, and practice doing the questions in the time that you will be given. See Handout 11.4: Procrastination Busters for more information about timers and how they can help you study.

5. Add to this list other suggestions from teachers, friends, and other sources.

On test day

1. Quickly write down any formulas, dates, or other memorized information you may need before you begin. (Only do this if you are 100 percent certain that this strategy will not be judged as cheating. I have heard stories of students who are not allowed to write anything but answers on their test papers.)

2. *Carefully* read directions, pay attention to any extra instructions from your teacher, and ask questions if you have them.

3. Quickly look over the whole test before you begin so that you can make sure not to spend too much time on any one question.

4. Expect that you will forget some things. Don't sweat it. If it happens, move on to other questions, and be confident that the information will come back to you as you continue working through the test.

5. If you are feeling very anxious, inhale while you slowly count to 4, and exhale while you count to 4. (If you want more ideas about how to regularly practice deep breathing, do an internet search and see which techniques and recommendations work best for you.)

6. Remind yourself that you are prepared, and that you can do this.

7. Add to this list other suggestions from teachers, friends, and other sources.

After the test

1. Congratulate yourself for doing your best and give yourself some kind of reward.

2. Once you get the test back, take a closer look at how you did and what you can do better next time, using Handout 11.5: Exam Wrappers.*

3. If you were really disappointed with how you did on the test and feel scared about looking at it, use Handout 9.5: A Process for Dealing with Negative Feedback or Failure to help yourself ease into it.

4. If your tests are not returned to you, then as soon as possible after you receive your grade, ask your teacher to meet with you. Explain that you would like to see which questions you answered incorrectly so that you can do better on the next test. At the meeting, take detailed notes about the questions you missed. Then do Handout 11.5: Exam Wrappers, using your notes.

* A learning strategist named Marsha Lovett at Carnegie Mellon University created this technique.

Study Tools Guide

Study Tools: What to Do During Focused Study Sessions

This guide is an expanded version of Handout 6.5: Quick Reference List of Study Tools. It lists study activities that you can do during your Focused Study Sessions. I have chosen the ones that are popular with students I know, but please keep in mind that there are other useful study tools that do not appear on this list. If you want some more ideas, talk to your teachers. Your friends might have additional ideas.

Please be aware that there are ideas and examples here for a wide range of levels, from freshmen all the way to seniors, in order to make it useful for the most students. If you are just starting high school, don't worry if some of the examples seem difficult. Just focus on using the learning strategies, and in a few years, you'll understand everything in this packet.

1. Making Flashcards

Flashcards are perfect for memorizing information like vocabulary words, names, dates, geographical facts, and formulas. Making flashcards by hand with index cards can be fun, but you can also use flashcard-making software that you can find online.

2. Taking Notes While You Read

There are many different ways to take notes, so if you don't already have a system that works, you may have to try out several different ways in order to find out what works best for you

Note-taking Method #1: Taking Notes While You Paraphrase

The first note-taking method I'll suggest is based on the reading strategy you've already learned: Put What You Are Reading into Your Own Words. I'll briefly remind you how it works. Let's say you are reading a section of a textbook. Using this method, you start at the beginning and read the first paragraph. Then you summarize what you've just read in your own words, either out loud or in your head. Next you read the second paragraph and put it into your own words *as you also fold in information from paragraph 1*, again, either out loud or in your head. Next you read the third paragraph and put it into your own words, *as you also fold in information from paragraphs 1 and 2*. You continue in this way until the end of the section, and when the next section begins, you start fresh with only the first paragraph of that section. The point of this method is to make sure you understand each section *as a whole* and are able to see the big picture and access deeper insights whenever you read. It's a way of getting you to higher levels of learning (see Handout 4.5).

But how does this method work with note-taking? As you put what you are reading into your own words, write some or all of it down. You will be adding new *information* and new *insights* into your written notes as you progress through the material, even though you will be paraphrasing from the beginning of the section. That's it.

Note-taking Method #2: Outlining

Another, slightly more advanced option is to take notes by outlining. With this method, you use traditional Roman numerals (I, II, III) to represent the broadest organizational level of information, capital letters (A, B, C) to represent the next level, and numbers (1, 2, 3) for the next level.

Has an English teacher ever asked you to outline a big writing project in this way? This is like doing that, but backwards. It's like playing detective to imagine what outline the textbook writer was using when they wrote the book. Making an outline can give you deep insight into how the information you are trying to learn is structured and organized. Outlining can get even more detailed, so if this technique appeals to you, go ahead and do an internet search to learn more about it.

Note-taking Method #3: Cornell Notes

If you want to take note-taking one step further, you can do an internet search on the Cornell note-taking system. It's a system developed by learning specialist named Walter Pauk. Two helpful videos appear on website of Cornell University's Learning Strategies Center, and I recommend you start with them.

If You Don't Know Which Method to Try, Keep It Simple

Remember you can always start with method #1 and jot things down as you paraphrase. Or just take free-form notes.

You Can Doodle or Sketch as You Take Notes

Whichever way you decide to do take notes, don't forget about the value of making little drawings while you take notes, especially if you like to doodle. If there are ideas or information that are easier to represent with a picture or a little graph, just go ahead and draw it. For example, if you're studying the French Revolution, "Maximilien Robespierre masterminded the Reign of Terror from 1792-1794 before being executed at the guillotine in 1794" is just as clearly expressed by "M. Robespierre ➔ Reign of Terror 1792-1794. MR 🪦 😵 in 1794." Doodles and drawings can also be useful in math and science classes when you have to draw models, graphs, or molecular structure. Of course, writing more fleshed-out notes can help you practice important skills if your tests involve short-answer or essay questions.

Pen & Paper or Keyboard?

Finally, there's the question of whether to take notes by hand or use a keyboard or other digital device. There are good arguments for both, so experiment and see what seems to work best for you. Taking notes by hand may be better for learning because it forces you to put things into your own words. But typed notes may be easier to review later. Of course, it matters if *you* have a big preference for one over the other because if you really dislike taking notes in a particular way, you'll be less likely to do it, no matter how good it might be for learning. You should feel free to use the method you prefer.

The bottom line is: always do what you think will work best for you, and stay open to trying other options if you find your first choice isn't working the way you want it to.

3. Highlighting

If your reading assignments are online or digital, it is often possible to highlight the text in different colors. If you are reading books or handouts, and you know you definitely have permission to mark them up, then you can use highlighter pens of different colors. For example, if you are learning about the Civil War in U.S. History, you might highlight the names of all Union politicians and military officials in blue and use a different color for those in the Confederacy. Color coding can be an efficient way to remind yourself how information is organized into different categories. One note of caution: don't use highlighting as a way of passively marking information "to learn later on." Instead, use it to actively support your use of the reading strategies.

4. Using Visuals: Mind Maps, Charts, Tables, and Timelines

Mind Maps

Mind mapping, or concept mapping, is a popular way of organizing information that may be harder to represent by writing lines of words. Mind mapping allows you to represent information, ideas, or events visually, and even in pictures. A mind map is created by putting the main concept or topic in the center of your map and then drawing branches from the central topic to several main ideas about the topic. You can continue drawing branches from each of the main ideas, and you can even represent connections between ideas with additional arrows.

Diagram B.1 shows a map of the Civil Rights Movement that a junior or senior might make while studying for an American history class. The main ideas branching off from the central idea are (1) the circumstances and conditions that led to the movement, (2) major activist events, (3) important court cases, (4) federal legislation that resulted, and (5) a selection of important organizations and figures. The student who created this map had to reach level 4 of Bloom's pyramid, *Analyzing*, in order to organize events from different time periods into overarching categories. *Having* the map is useful for review, but *creating* the map is what allows this student to enjoy the deep, secure learning that will enable them to excel on a test.

What if a student is taking an advanced class like AP U.S. History and needs to include much more detail in their study materials? In that case, online or digital maps are a good choice because they hold unlimited information. Use them for more advanced classes.

Diagram B.1 doesn't contain any images within the map, but mind maps can be particularly great for more visual subjects like geography, biology, or chemistry, where you need to draw lots of molecules, cell components, organs, or other anatomical features.

Charts and Graphs

Ways of visualizing information other than mind maps include flowcharts, bar charts, pie charts, and graphs. Flowcharts are helpful when you want to lay out a process, or something that happens in sequence. They can be useful in science and history classes, and you can also use them for laying out the plots of novels or other kinds of stories. Diagram B.2 shows a flowchart for the process of meiosis, which every high school biology student will need to master at some point. Diagram B.3 shows a bar chart of the gases in Earth's atmosphere, which all earth science students will eventually be tested on. Making charts is a powerful way of helping you learn the information deeply so that it will be there whenever you're asked about it on a test.

Graphs are also great for deep learning. An algebra student might find it very helpful to make a review sheet comparing the graphs for a line ($y = x$), a parabola ($y = x2$), a cubic ($y = x3$), and even higher powers of x. Then they could add some examples of translations ($y = x2 + b$) and dilations ($y = ax3$) and be able to see what the patterns are and how they work.

Tables

Tables are a very popular choice for organizing information. Diagram B.4 shows one for an upper-level English class and Diagram B.5 shows one for an algebra II or pre-calculus class.

Studying a novel is a great opportunity to use a table, as demonstrated by Diagram B.4. The student who created this table had to get to Bloom's level 4, *Analyzing*, in order to create it. Because the student had the goal of creating the table as she read, she took more thoughtful notes and engaged in deeper metacognition. So the table activated her learning in several ways. Having Diagram B.4 as a review tool before a test is just icing on the cake for this student.

Diagram B.5 shows how a table can be used to map out different approaches to solving trigonometric identities. A student using the homework strategy (Handout 6.2) could create this study tool over the course of two or three weeks, as they move through the unit, do more and more of these kinds of problems, and have more *aha* moments. Even after creating the table in its current form, the student can continue filling it in and refining it. But be aware that there are lots of different ways to organize the information in Diagram B.5. The diagram only shows one way. You should always do what feels right for you and the way your brain works!

In short, making tables is as useful as making maps, charts, or graphs when it comes to climbing Bloom's pyramid to higher levels of learning. The act of organizing the information is a powerful metacognitive process that will help your brain remember what it needs when you're taking tests.

Timelines

Finally, timelines are great for learning history, whether it's for an actual history class, for a historical novel in English class, or a sequence of events like the development of atomic models. You can find examples of a timeline in any history textbook or by doing an internet search for timelines.

With all of these visual tools, you have the choice between making your images by hand on paper or going digital and using software and apps. Whatever floats your boat. Ask your friends and teacher for recommendations, experiment, and stay open to your instincts and creativity.

Mapping the Civil Rights Movement

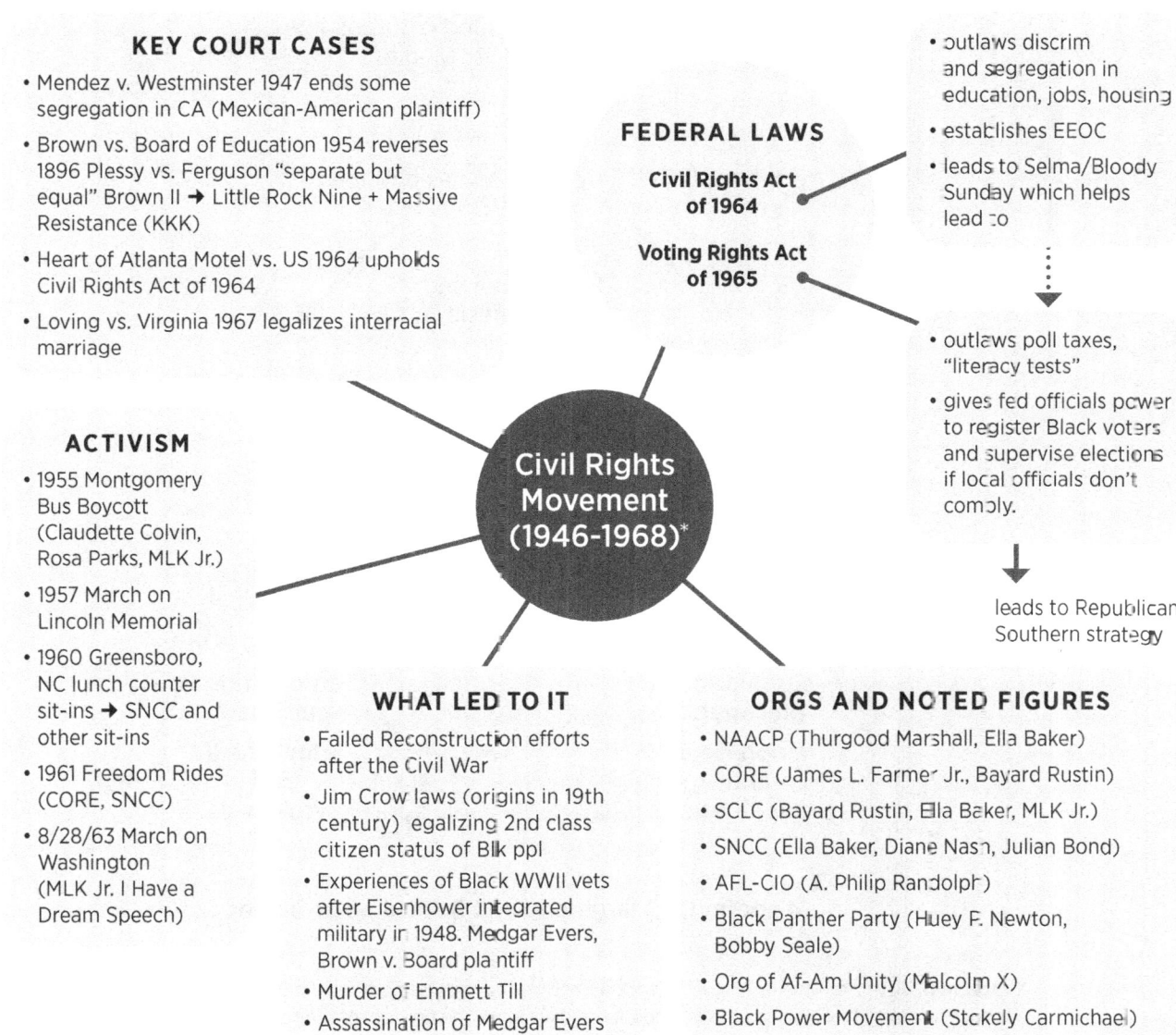

KEY COURT CASES

- Mendez v. Westminster 1947 ends some segregation in CA (Mexican-American plaintiff)
- Brown vs. Board of Education 1954 reverses 1896 Plessy vs. Ferguson "separate but equal" Brown II ➔ Little Rock Nine + Massive Resistance (KKK)
- Heart of Atlanta Motel vs. US 1964 upholds Civil Rights Act of 1964
- Loving vs. Virginia 1967 legalizes interracial marriage

ACTIVISM

- 1955 Montgomery Bus Boycott (Claudette Colvin, Rosa Parks, MLK Jr.)
- 1957 March on Lincoln Memorial
- 1960 Greensboro, NC lunch counter sit-ins ➔ SNCC and other sit-ins
- 1961 Freedom Rides (CORE, SNCC)
- 8/28/63 March on Washington (MLK Jr. I Have a Dream Speech)

FEDERAL LAWS

Civil Rights Act of 1964

Voting Rights Act of 1965

- outlaws discrim and segregation in education, jobs, housing
- establishes EEOC
- leads to Selma/Bloody Sunday which helps lead to

- outlaws poll taxes, "literacy tests"
- gives fed officials power to register Black voters and supervise elections if local officials don't comply.

leads to Republican Southern strategy

Civil Rights Movement (1946-1968)*

WHAT LED TO IT

- Failed Reconstruction efforts after the Civil War
- Jim Crow laws (origins in 19th century) egalizing 2nd class citizen status of Blk ppl
- Experiences of Black WWII vets after Eisenhower integrated military in 1948. Medgar Evers, Brown v. Board pla ntiff
- Murder of Emmett Till
- Assassination of Medgar Evers

ORGS AND NOTED FIGURES

- NAACP (Thurgood Marshall, Ella Baker)
- CORE (James L. Farmer Jr., Bayard Rustin)
- SCLC (Bayard Rustin, Ella Baker, MLK Jr.)
- SNCC (Ella Baker, Diane Nash, Julian Bond)
- AFL-CIO (A. Philip Randolph)
- Black Panther Party (Huey F. Newton, Bobby Seale)
- Org of Af-Am Unity (Malcolm X)
- Black Power Movement (Stokely Carmichael)

*some sources limit to 1954-1968

Diagram B.1. An example of a mind map for a junior- or senior-level history class. In order to make this map, this student must create an overview of the Civil Rights Movement, sorting events from various time periods into different categories like "Federal Laws" or "Key Court Cases." This mind map on 8.5 x 11-inch paper is limited in how much detail it shows, but on ine or digital maps can hold unlimited information and are useful for more advanced classes. A timeline would be another great tool for learning this material.

Meiosis Flowchart

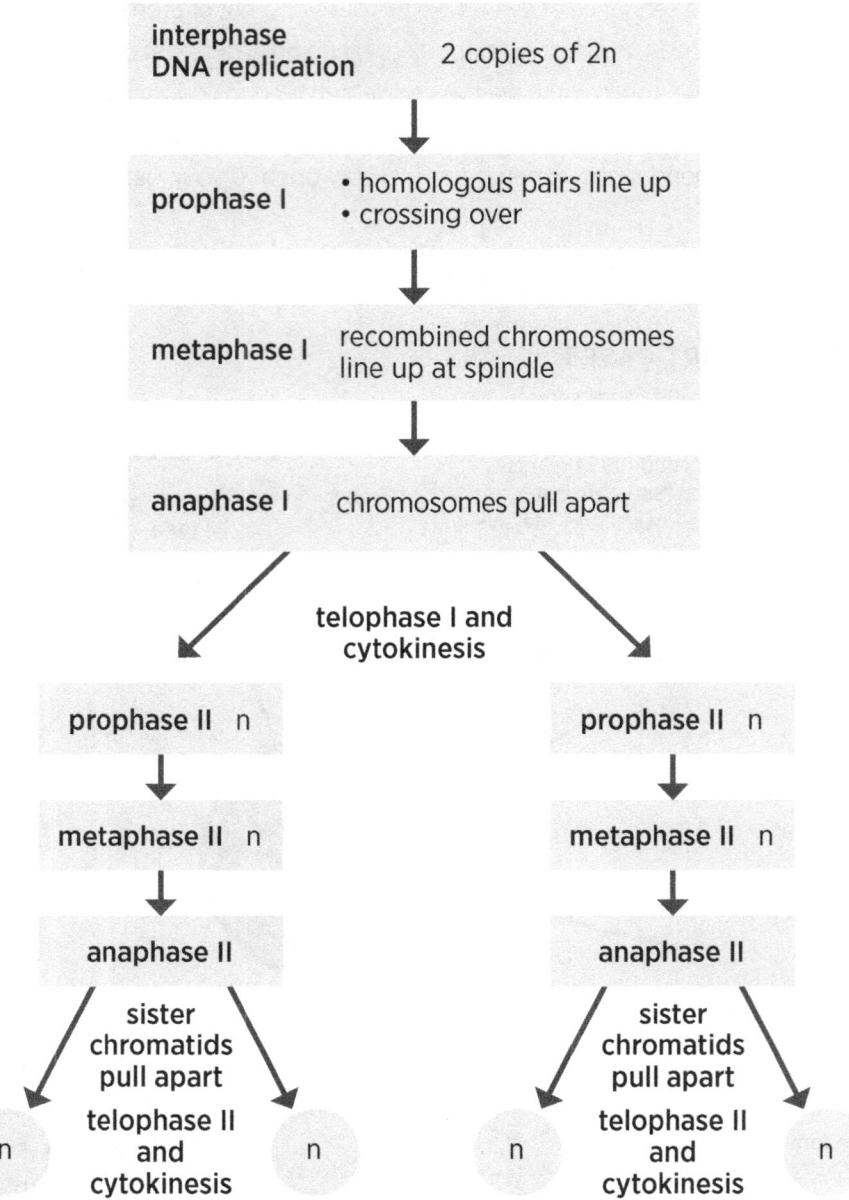

4 sperm OR 1 large egg and 3 small polar bodies

Diagram B.2. An example of a flowchart for a freshman- or sophomore-level biology class. Making this chart without referring to notes helps this student securely learn the process of meiosis.

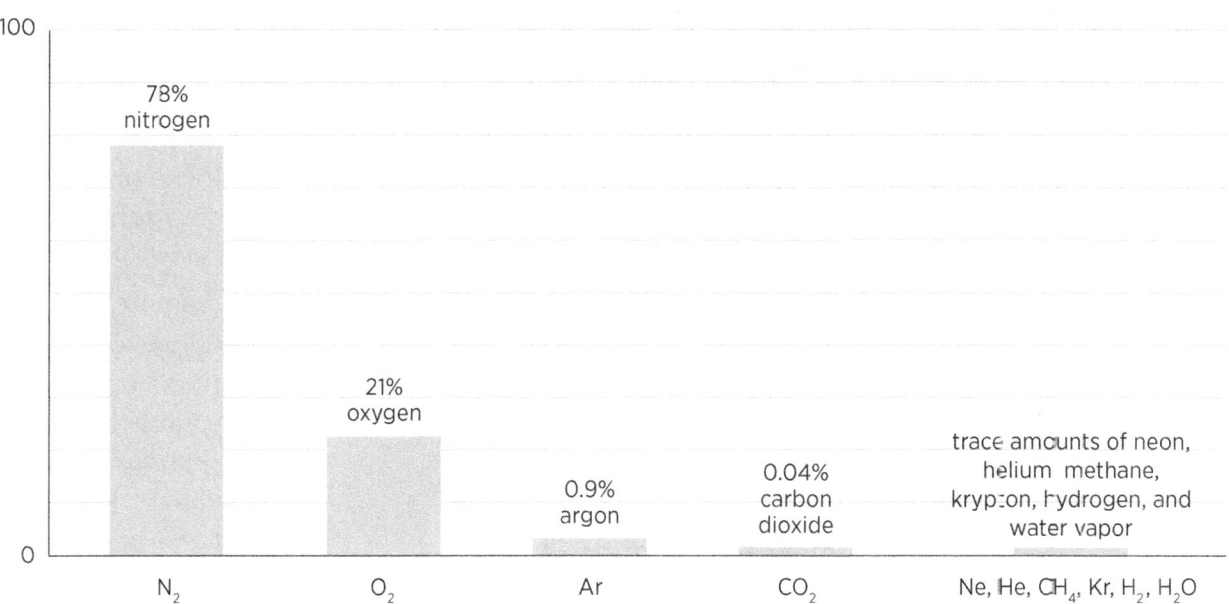

Bar Chart of Earth's Atmospheric Composition

Diagram B.3. An example of a bar chart for a freshman- or sophomore-level earth science class. Making the chart helps the student learn the information securely, and they also have it as a review sheet.

PARTIAL BREAKDOWN OF *PLAGUE OF DOVES* BY LOUISE ERDRICH, SET IN THE FICTIONAL TOWN OF PLUTO, NORTH DAKOTA

NARRATORS & PERSPECTIVES	SYMBOLS & THEMES	LITERARY & HISTORICAL REFS	BACKGROUNDS & LANGUAGES
Generation born ~1950 • Evelina Harp Generation born ~1915 • Judge Antone Coutts • Marn Wolde Generation born ~1890 • Cordelia Lochren Generation born ~1870 • Joseph Coutts • Shamengwa • Mooshum/Seraph Milk (narrates through others' accounts of his storytelling) 3rd person omniscient • Warren Wolde, Billy Peace • John Wildstrand (through Antone Coutts) Others?	Reptiles/Amphibians • salamanders (bred by Harps in backyard pond, almost-killer of Father Cassidy, Evelina's college hallucinations) • Sister Mary Anita called Godzilla by students • Marn Wolde's snake handling symbols of both damnation and salvation Music/Violin • witness to 1888 murders • bond between Henri and Lafayette and their downfall • savior of Joseph Coutts during prospecting winter • savior of Shamengwa and then Corwin Peace • killer of Warren Wolde Religion/Spirituality • Roman Catholicism • Indigenous spiritual traditions • born-again Christianity • new age spirituality • Mormonism • agnostic (Sister Mary Anita)	Greeks & Romans Marcus Aurelius (read by Joseph Coutts, then Antone Coutts, then Evelina) Lucretius Epicetus Plotinus Modern Writers (all Evelina) • Anaïs Nin • Albert Camus • Arthur Rimbaud • Sylvia Plath Historical References • Louis Riel (as Michif visionary hero, or as misguided, or as a source of Milk family's and Lafayette's credibility/respect many others. ask for help with this in class.	Backgrounds • Métis (many characters, see below) • French/Chippewa (Evelina, younger Harps, younger Coutts, Henri, Lafayette) • Chippewa (Milk family) • Cree • Dakota • German • Norwegian Languages • English • Ojibwe • Michif • French Michif - different? • French • German

Diagram B.4. An example of a table for junior- or senior-level English class analyzing the novel *The Plague of Doves* by Louise Erdrich. The student uses the table to organize the different narrators and themes of the book, operating at level 4 of Bloom's pyramid of learning.

Solving Trig Identities

Formulas for Solving Identities (memorize all formulas with flashcards)

- reciprocal identities   example: $1/\sin\theta = \csc\theta$
- Pythagorean identities   example: $\sin^2\theta + \cos^2\theta = 1$
- complementary identities   example: $\cos(\theta - 90) = \sin\theta$
- sum and difference identities   example: $\sin(A \pm B) = \sin A \cos B \pm \cos A \sin B$
- double and half angle identities example: $\cos^2 A = \cos^2 A - \sin^2 A$
- law of sines
- law of cosines
- algebraic identities   examples: $(a + b)^2 = a^2 + 2ab + b^2$
                                              OR $(a+b)^3 = (a + b)(a^2 - ab + b^2)$

Approaches for Solving Identities

IF	THEN
there are squares, cubes, or other powers	try Pythagorean, double angle, or algebraic identities or the cosine rule, depending on what it most looks like
there are angles angle like 75 or 135 (or any angle that's a sum or difference of the common angles)	try one of the sum and difference identities
the expression is similar to the law of sines or the law of cosines	try whichever law it looks like
the expression is similar to an algebraic identity	try whichever one it looks like
there are square roots	try half-angle identities
you get stuck or don't know what to do	convert everything to sines and cosines
you get stuck or don't know what to do	can you convert to a complementary angle?
(general tip)	pick one side to work with, but be aware you might need to work with the other side too
(general tip)	don't move terms from one side to another

Diagram B. 5. An example of a student combining a list and chart to learn how to solve trig identities in a junior- or senior-level class. The *list* shows all the different kinds of formulas they must memorize, at level 1 of Bloom's. The *chart*, however, is level 3 of Bloom's. *Applying*.

5. Making Study Guides

Study guides are great for reviewing information that you have learned over a period of weeks or months while using the other tools. That makes it ideal for test preparation.

Two popular formats for study guides are (1) outlines and (2) tables (sometimes called charts). With both formats, you organize the information from the entire unit into one outline or table. The task of combining and integrating the information makes you go to higher levels of learning on Bloom's pyramid.

You also have the option to create a study guide simply by combining the outlines, maps, tables, charts, or graphs that you created during the unit or chapter. But you may find that your understanding has grown as the unit progressed, and so you need to revise or add to your earlier materials. That revision is a very valuable part of the learning process.

Many textbooks have *learning objectives* or *learning goals* at the beginning or end of every chapter. They may not be labeled with those terms, but they will be introduced with language like, "By the end of this chapter you should be able to..." You can use them to organize your study guides. Turn the objectives into questions, and make sure you have information in your study guide that addresses all of the questions. For example, if your book says: By the end of this chapter you should be able to:

- Explain the states of matter
- Convert grams to moles
- Describe different types of bonding

then your questions would look like this:

- What are the states of matter?
- What is the procedure for converting grams to moles?
- What are all the different types of bonds?

and the section of your study guide for just the *first* question would look like this:

I.   Chapter 1: Matter, Interactions, and Reactions

    A.   Three States of Matter

        1.   Gases: atoms or molecules are far apart, interactions are weak. Gases fill their containers. Examples are water vapor- $H_2O(g)$, methane- $CH_4(g)$, and nitrogen- $N_2(g)$.

        2.   Liquids: atoms or molecules are closer together, interactions are stronger than in gases, weaker than in solids. Liquids take the shape of their containers. Examples are water- $H_2O(l)$, octane- $C_8H_{18}(l)$, and mercury $Hg(l)$.

        3.   Solids: atoms or molecules are very close together, interactions are stronger than in liquids. Solids maintain their shape. Examples are table salt- $NaCl(s)$, calcium carbonate- $CaCO_3(s)$, and diamond- $C(s)$.

Here is an example of a study guide that isn't as helpful:

I.   Chapter 1: Matter, Interactions, and Reactions

A.   Know the states of matter

B.   Know how to convert grams to moles

C.   Know the different types of bonding

Although this attempt at a study guide is better than doing nothing, and it makes the student who created it *feel* like they're studying, they're not really engaging deeply with the information so that they can really *learn* it. To get the most out of making study guides, fill them with useful information, and then make sure you can teach that information.

6. Using Mnemonic Devices

Mnemonic device is just a fancy term for a trick that helps you remember something. The name Roy G. Biv is one example. It represents the colors of the rainbow: Red, Orange, Yellow, Green, Blue, Indigo, and Violet. The first letter of each of the colors spells Roy G. Biv. A second example: Dear King Philip Came Over for Great Spaghetti. The first letter of each word in the sentence matches the first letter of each of the taxonomic levels that biology students have to learn: domain, kingdom, phylum, class, order, family, genus, species. The nonsense word IPMAT could help you remember the phases of mitosis: interphase, prophase, metaphase, anaphase, and telophase. Whenever you have to memorize a list of some kind, see if you can come up with a mnemonic device to help you.

7. Creating Practice Quizzes and Tests, with or without Apps

You can use past homework assignments, quizzes, and extra textbook questions to try to create your own practice test. This is an advanced study strategy, but it can work really well. A slightly easier option is to use an app to quiz yourself with flashcards that you've already made.

However, as long as you do your homework in the way that I've suggested, you will be regularly testing yourself.

Keep it Simple: Focus on One to Three Tools that Work for You

OK, so now I've given you everything I've got. I've laid out all of these study tools so that you have options, because I never want learning to feel like torture or drudgery for you. But please don't feel overwhelmed by all these choices. Using *only one* study tool—for example, perhaps taking notes—could really be all you need to totally transform your learning. Just choose something to do during your Focused Study Sessions that you feel excited to try.

If you find it doesn't work the way you were hoping it would, no worries! You can just try another tool. It's all about what works best for *you* and your learning process. That's what metacognition—thinking about thinking—is all about.

Of course, if you want to go for broke and use all the variations of all seven tools, go for it!

Now, a couple of questions for you:

1. What note-taking strategies or tools have you used up to this point? Feel free to include tools that may not be listed in this guide.

2. What note-taking strategies and tools from this guide do you think you might want to try in the future?

Final Note: Why Memorizing Is Still Important Even Though We Want to Go to Higher Learning Levels

Your parent or mentor has explained to you why it's important not to get stuck at the bottom of the pyramid of learning levels by *only* memorizing. But you might be asking yourself: Why do I have to memorize anything at all if I have the internet at my fingertips? The answer is that we can only think creatively with the information we have in our heads. Memorizing is the foundation of learning. That's why it's at the bottom of the pyramid. Everything rests upon it. So it's extremely valuable to learn to do simple math in your head or to memorize vocabulary words, history dates, or literary terms, for example.

My older daughter is a doctor and a professor. Once she asked a student if it was wise to give pregnant women a drug that acts like adrenaline. She expected him to think hard about it, but instead he just looked it up on the internet and answered, "No." But he couldn't tell her *why* that was the right answer. Later, when he thought about it, he realized it was obvious that a drug that makes blood vessels smaller is not a good idea for a woman carrying a child. If he had taken the time to *memorize* (pyramid level 1) the effects of adrenaline, then he could have *applied* (level 3) that knowledge immediately. He would have realized that, because a pregnant woman's blood vessels need to deliver blood to both herself and the baby, anything that acts like adrenaline would not be good for her. Now let me ask you: Would you rather have a doctor who looks up everything on the internet, focusing on questions of *what* instead of *why*, or a doctor who can think creatively on the spot, quickly add new information to their understanding, and come up with solutions to help you feel better?

If you would prefer the second type of doctor, I hope you will feel inspired to lay the important groundwork of memorizing so that you can eventually have a lot of fun climbing to the very top of Bloom's pyramid of learning. No matter what field you decide to go into—the arts, business, technical fields, law, or any number of other areas—when you've taken the time to memorize the basics, you can start to think creatively. And *that's* when you can start to contribute new and valuable innovations and insights to your field. As you soar, you will be helping humanity meet the challenges of the day.

Keep Handout 6.5 handy as a quick reference of study tools.

List of Handouts

Note: The first number in each handout name is the chapter that the handout belongs to.

NAME	TITLE
Handout 3.1	Who is Dr. McGuire and Why Should I Care About What She Says?
Handout 3.2	What is Metacognition and How Can It Help Me?
Handout 3.3	Count the Vowels
Handout 3.4	Metacognition Worksheet
Handout 4.1	Answering Reflection Questions
Handout 4.2	Other Students' Answers to Reflection Question #1
Handout 4.3	Other Students' Answers to Reflection Question #3
Handout 4.4	Alternative Answers to Reflection Question #3
Handout 4.5	Bloom's Levels of Learning
Handout 4.6	Bloom's Levels of Learning: Goldilocks Edition
Handout 5.1	The Study Cycle
Handout 5.2	Focused Study Sessions
Handout 5.3	The Study Cycle and Focused Study Sessions Combined
Handout 6.1	Guess the Activity/The Power of Previewing
Handout 6.2	Using Your Homework to Test Your Understanding
Handout 6.3	Ten Learning Strategies
Handout 6.4	Learning Strategies Worksheet
Handout 6.5	Quick Reference: List of Study Tools
Handout 7.1	Fixed and Growth Mindsets
Handout 7.2	Mindset Worksheet

(continued)

NAME	TITLE
Handout 8.2	Worksheet about My Interests and Things I Enjoy Doing
Handout 8.3	How Do You Prefer to Learn? (Worksheet)
Handout 8.4	How to Figure Out What You Are Actually Supposed to Be Doing
Handout 8.5	Self-Talk Journaling Worksheet
Handout 8.6	Doing What *You* Can and Letting Go of the Rest (Worksheet)
Handout 9.2	Dealing with Setbacks, Mistakes, and Failure
Handout 9.3	Stumbling Blocks or Stepping-Stones?
Handout 9.4	Mistakes and Failure Worksheet
Handout 9.5	A Process for Dealing with Negative Feedback or Failure
Handout 9.6	Worksheet—Defining Success
Handout 10.1	Study Preferences Worksheet
Handout 10.2	Study Session Checklist
Handout 10.3	Rocks in a Bucket
Handout 10.4	Filling Out Your Term Calendar
Handout 10.5	Filling Out Your Week Calendar
Handout 10.6	App Detox Worksheet
Handout 10.7	Quiz: Saying No, Setting Boundaries, and Protecting Your Time
Handout 11.1	Worksheet: What Gets You Fired Up Deep Down Inside?
Handout 11.2	Mapping Out Your Year
Handout 11.3	Getting the Most out of a Syllabus
Handout 11.4	Procrastination Busters
Handout 11.5	Exam Wrappers
Handout 11.6	Learning Strategies Inventory
Handout 11.7	Strategies and Tools Tracker
Handout 11.8	When Overwhelm Strikes
Handout 11.9	Quick Reference List of All Learning Support Resources
Handout 12.1	Core Content
Handout 12.2	Additional Content
Appendix A	Test Preparation Guide
Appendix B	Study Tools Guide

About the Authors

Saundra Yancy McGuire, PhD is an internationally acclaimed learning specialist who has been teaching students strategies for improving their learning for more than fifty years. She was named a 2022 Louisiana Legend by Louisiana Public Broadcasting for her numerous national awards. In 2007, she was recognized for excellence in mentoring with a Presidential Award presented in a White House Oval Office Ceremony. She is also an elected Fellow of the American Association for the Advancement of Science (2011), the American Chemical Society (2010), and the Council of Learning Assistance and Developmental Education Associations (2012). In 2013 she retired as Assistant Vice Chancellor and Professor of Chemistry at Louisiana State University, and in 2017 she was inducted into the LSU College of Science Hall of Distinction. She is now Professor Emerita of Chemistry and Director Emerita of the LSU Center for Academic Success, which was recognized by the National College Learning Center Association as the nation's most outstanding learning center in 2004 and is currently designated as a national Learning Center of Excellence. Saundra has presented her widely acclaimed learning strategies workshops at more than 500 institutions in forty-seven states and thirteen countries. She received her B.S. degree, magna cum laude, from Southern University in Baton Rouge, LA, her Master's degree from Cornell University, and her Ph.D. from the University of Tennessee at Knoxville, where she received the Chancellor's Citation for Exceptional Professional Promise. She is married to Physics Professor Emeritus Stephen C. McGuire, and they are the parents of Dr. Carla McGuire Davis and Dr. Stephanie McGuire and the doting grandparents of Joshua, Ruth, Daniel, and Joseph Davis.

Stephanie McGuire holds a bachelor's degree in biology from Massachusetts Institute of Technology, master's and doctoral degrees in neuroscience from the University of Oxford, and a master's degree in opera performance from the Longy Conservatory. She attended Oxford on a Marshall scholarship and received a graduate fellowship from the National Science Foundation. Partly as a result of long and stimulating conversations with her mother about pedagogy and learning strategies, Stephanie became a highly sought-after private academic tutor in the New York City area where she lived for ten years. By coauthoring this book, she is delighted to contribute to Dr. Saundra McGuire's admirable and revolutionary mission to make all students expert learners. Since graduating from conservatory, Stephanie has enjoyed forging a successful career as a classical mezzo-soprano. She has performed with the New York City Opera at Lincoln Center, with the Boston POPS Orchestra in Symphony Hall and several times at Carnegie Hall. She now lives in Berlin.